Johnson's eloquent portra, hood to adulthood are gripping in their stark realities. From the prologue to the last page, she shares the hopes she and her family had coming to America for a better life. There is an eloquence in her retelling her tale. Most likely too many women will relate to her challenges.

— Emil Toth, *Author of Love's Transformation, Love's Sacrifice, Love's Wisdom & Seven Souls on a Cross*

What an impressive, heartrending and inspiring story of struggle, endurance and overcoming adversity.

— Dr. Ronald R. Blanck, Lieutenant General, US Army (Retired), Former Army Surgeon General

A very compelling story that could have been a tragedy except for the courage, intellect, and self-awareness of an Arab girl who transformed herself into an American success as a woman, nurse, and Army officer.

— Nancy R. Adams RN, MSN, FAAN Major General US Army (Retired), 19th Chief, Army Nurse Corps

Mona's determination to overcome the trauma she endured as a child from a mother who did not know how to love her and the physical, emotional and financial abuses suffered as a young wife kept drawing me back to her story. Her belief in love and knowing love was the right focus of her life demonstrated her innate ability to persist and thrive. An emotionally difficult read that offers hope.

— Gale S. Pollock, CRNA, FACHE, FAAN, Major General, US Army (Retired), Elevivo LLC, Pollock Associates, LLC

NOT CREATED EQUAL

NOT CREATED EQUAL

AN IMMIGRANT MUSLIM WOMAN'S PURSUIT OF EQUALITY IN HER FAMILY, THE ARMY AND AMERICA

MONA JOHNSON
Lieutenant Colonel, US Army (Retired)

MonaJohnsonAuthor.com

Printed in the United States of America

Library of Congress Control Number - Pending

ISBN: 978-1-7347317-0-5 (print)

ISBN: 978-1-7347317-1-2(ebook)

Ordering Information:

Special discounts are available on quantity purchases by corporations,
associations, and others. For details, contact monajohnsonauthor@gmail.com

Dedication

✿ ✿ ✿

To my dear Vati. Without your guidance and example, I most certainly would not be who I am today and would perhaps be writing a whole different story.

One of your favorite quatrains from Omar Khayyam's

RUBAIYAT:

"The Moving Finger writes; and, having writ,

Moves on: nor all thy Piety nor Wit

Shall lure it back to cancel half a Line,

Nor all thy Tears wash out a Word of it."

"There is no greater agony than bearing an untold story inside you."

~ Maya Angelou

Disclaimers

This memoir is a work of creative nonfiction. I have reconstructed and portrayed the characters and events to the best of my memory and ability. Some events have been compressed and a few scenes are composites of events. Much of the information had been documented in public court records, military records, and calendar bullet diaries I kept throughout my adult life. In addition, the recollection of early events of my childhood and youth have been recreated based on oral history from various family members and friends of four generations as told to me. While all the stories and events in this book are true, some names and identifying details have been changed to protect the privacy of the people involved. Also, because no conversations can be remembered word for word verbatim, especially many years later, the basis of the dialogues in all instances although accurate, have been retold with the intention to capture and express the concepts, feelings, and emotions.

CONTENTS

PROLOGUE

Of all the decisions I had made over 29 years of life, the biggest and most important choice I made would be the result of an utterance from my toddler.

Three little words. Spoken to me in Arabic.

I had heard them before, but only from my husband, never from my little girl. I heard them when I suggested he help me cook dinner and during the agony of labor. I heard them nearly daily for several years to the point that they almost—*almost*—began to feel like a normal part of my life. Only from him, always from him.

Three little words.

Until one day, they came from her. A tiny voice, from a tiny body. But the message was clear.

"Ikhrassi ya bit." In English: Shut up, bitch.

In the seconds it took for me to register those words, almost as quickly as they left the tiny mouth from which they came, I knew. I had known for a long time, but now it was crystal clear. It was now or never. I had to get out.

I looked into her deep, brown eyes, full of wonder and innocence. *How did I get here?* I asked myself.

She knew what she'd said, but she didn't *really* know. She loved me, that much I knew. She'd never want to hurt me. Not like he did.

"Don't ever say that to Mommy again, sweetheart," I told her, as firmly and as gently as I could. "That's very hurtful."

"Sorry, Mommy," she replied.

I couldn't have known then how my life would change as a result of those three words, which were in the same utterance both meaningless and powerful. For nearly 30 years, when it came to the things that mattered in life, I had been told what to do, and I had dutifully obeyed all of the rules, the expectations, the quotes from the Qur'an. I had quelled the conflict in my heart between my cultural values and my independent spirit. Now I had no plan.

All I ever wanted was to live a good life, be treated fairly, be equal.

"What now?" I thought. "Who am I?"

PART I

*No one is where he is by accident,
and chance plays no part in God's plan.*

~ A Course in Miracles

CHAPTER 1

EXILED

Most people know Giza for its ancient pyramids. For me, it's a place faint in my memory, but it's special nonetheless. That Sunday in November 1951 was an ordinary day in Egypt. As Americans celebrated Veterans Day, Mutti gave birth to me, her second child.

Mutti is the German nickname for "mother," and mine was half-German. My grandfather, Abbas Hussein, was Egyptian, and as vice-consul in the Egyptian Embassy in Berlin, he met and married a shy German woman, Erna Ellerkmann, my grandmother. Though she made Cairo her home after she married my grandfather, she still identified strongly with her native country. Erna even crossed the ocean back to Germany each time she was pregnant so her children could have dual citizenship. She gave birth in 1924 to a girl, Aidi, then in 1926 a boy, Rolf. Inge, my mother, was the youngest of their three children, born in 1930. All three children were raised in Cairo with a good balance of their bicultural heritage. At the time, Egypt was still colonized by the British with a large Western influence imported by British, French, and German citizens.

My first six years of life include happy, albeit dim, memories of my native Egypt, complete with summer afternoons spent swimming under the hot North African sun at our local club in Heliopolis and winter celebrations of my grandmother's German heritage. Those celebrations included a Christmas tree my aunt Aidi, who lived in Switzerland, selected for my uncle Rolf, a commercial airline pilot, to transport to us. We were probably one of the few Muslim families in Egypt that celebrated Christmas, but it was a part of our culture, part of us. It was different from the Muslim holidays we observed, but even so, it suited our family.

My father's name was Ali Kamal Sakr, but at home we called him *Vati*, the German nickname for "father." I was told my father preferred to be called Vati so he could help reinforce my mother's German heritage. Vati was friendly and kind to everyone, whether he knew the person or not. He was by all accounts very handsome. Professionally, he had been a police officer, but by the time I was born, he was so much more than a cop on the beat: he'd earned a law degree from Cairo University and had become part of the group secretly plotting to overthrow the monarchy of King Farouk.

Among the group of army and police officers were Muhammad Naguib, Gamal Abdel Nasser, and Vati's good friend, Anwar Sadat. They called themselves the Free Officers, and their mission was to drive Farouk and the British out of Egypt and bring the country into self-governance.

They succeeded. In July 1952, the Free Officers led the Egyptian Revolution of 1952, a bloodless CIA backed coup that sent Farouk into exile. Egypt declared itself a republic, and eventually, Nasser became its second president. Although he was hugely popular with the public at large, Nasser's secret actions were a cause for alarm at the highest levels of government. Many of the Free

Officers had been elevated to important positions in the cabinet, but Nasser was always looking over his shoulder, convinced that his former colleagues were conspiring against him, either plotting to overthrow him, place him under house arrest (as he did to Muhammad Naguib), or planning his assassination. As his paranoia increased, he began having them imprisoned and tortured for various false allegations. Vati tried to spare me specific details, but the facts were still objectively horrible, as he recalled the times he witnessed prisoners being beaten, burned with hot oil or gasoline, hanged, or attacked by dogs.

For Vati, now a high-ranking police official, this was a crisis of conscience. The men Nasser was after were innocent men. Many of them were Vati's friends, and despite the danger, he released them after they'd been arrested.

It was only a matter of time before Vati's actions were discovered. Nasser saw this as treason, a crime punishable by death. I was six years old when Anwar Sadat came to our home to warn my father that his arrest was imminent. Hearing the two murmur in another room, I assumed this was just another visit. Then Vati left the house hurriedly and, I learned later, escaped from Egypt and took refuge in Saudi Arabia. I cried for days waiting for his return.

"He's not that far away, and he'll be home shortly," Mutti said, in an effort to console me.

To me, he may as well have gone to the moon. I didn't see him for what seemed like forever, even though in reality it was only a few months.

Then one day, Vati suddenly showed up at home—he'd risked his own life to spirit the rest of us out of the country. Our *Onkel* Rolf, Mutti's pilot brother, helped Vati. I was afraid and confused hearing the adults' frantic voices, German mixed with Arabic, including those of my grandparents, who lived nearby. The sudden bustling and hurried movements around me were a stark contrast to the quiet life we enjoyed just moments before. We packed lightly and quickly, since my parents were told there were only a few minutes to get us out. Mutti told me I could bring only a few clothing items with me because there wasn't much room in my tiny suitcase. When I packed my dolly and her clothes, Mutti's stern voice rose behind me. "Only your clothes and shoes. No dolly or toys!" Tears welled up in my eyes. We had to leave everything and everyone else behind.

"*Meine Puppe, meine Puppe!*" I couldn't stop crying out for my doll, even as we were rushed out of the house. It was the last time I ever saw my grandfather and it would be several years before I saw my grandmother again.

Onkel Rolf made sure there would be no record of Vati coming in or out of the country. As we raced to the airport, tension filled the car as I imagined who might try to stop us. Piecing together bits of words here and there, I wondered if we were going to die.

It was my first introduction to an airport. I wore my newest light blue dress and white shoes, since air travel was considered an occasion to dress up as if we were going to church. Onkel Rolf waited for us as the flight boarded. He took us from the ramp and straight onto the aircraft. There's no doubt that others were involved in helping Onkel Rolf but I will never know their names.

When the wheels lifted off the runway, my parents let out a sigh of relief and by extension, I would never feel as relieved to take off into the sky than I was that day. My first flight ever had turned out to be so exasperating for my parents, and it remained an indelible memory for me.

Saudi Arabia and a New Islam

The Islam my father taught me is the Islam I still follow today. One of my clearest childhood memories is sitting with him in our living room in Cairo as he introduced me and my oldest brother, Tarek, to the fundamental principles of Islam. Very informally, yet gracefully, he taught us that one only had to submit himself or herself to God to be a Muslim and to believe that there is only one God and that Muhammed ("PBUH," he would add) was his last messenger. That was it! His simple definition rings in my ears today as I observe and often cringe at the many misconceptions floating around about our religion and the people who practice it. (PBUH stands for Peace Be Upon Him, or Her. Saying it after mentioning a prophet's name is customary in Islam and is a sign of respect that the soul be at peace.)

My father was devout. He also believed that a good Muslim knows not only the Qur'an but also the *Bible* and the *Torah* and honors all the prophets of the Old and New Testaments. He believed that learning about other religions is part of a well-rounded education and that education was empowering for all his children, including me, his only daughter. Within this tolerant, life-affirming faith, I grew up understanding that the decision to wear a *hijab, burqa, abaya,* or other covering is a choice each woman makes by herself and for herself. It is a voluntary spiritual gesture, not a restriction imposed upon her by either her government or her religion.

In 1957, I learned firsthand that not all Muslims shared this point of view. At the time, our family was living in Dhahran, Saudi Arabia. For the first few years of my childhood, we'd led a comfortable, upper middle class life in Cairo, which was already a bustling, cosmopolitan city. Most urban Egyptians wore Western clothing. All the women in my family dressed in modern styles and kept up with the latest fashions. They didn't cover their hair in public. On the streets of Cairo back then, few women did.

But in Dhahran, women were to be invisible as individual persons. Whenever a Saudi woman went out in public, or was in an environment where there were men not from her immediate family, she wore an *abaya*, a loose garment, usually black, that enveloped her from head to toe. A veil or *niqab* covered her face—nothing was to be exposed except her hands, feet, and eyes.

This dress code was zealously enforced by members of the religious police, or *mutawwa*. Small bands of pious young men stationed themselves on street corners, ready to confront anyone who, in their judgment, was violating Islam's codes of dress or conduct. They enforced dietary laws prohibiting the consumption of pork and alcoholic beverages and made sure that shops closed at prayer times. They also arrested nonrelated men and women caught socializing with one another or anyone suspected of engaging in prostitution or homosexual behavior. Above all, however, these self-appointed guardians of the faith were on the lookout for "indecent" women—women who were not wearing the *abaya*. They carried whips as a means of enforcement and used them to flog anyone they deemed in violation.

One morning, when I was six years old, I went on a routine walk with Mutti to the local *souk*, or market, to buy fresh fruits and vegetables. Mutti was dressed in a tasteful knee-length skirt and short-sleeved blouse, the same kind of clothing she'd worn in Cairo. A very young *mutawwa* challenged her from across the street. Holding his whip in one hand and pointing at her with the other, he called out, "Why are you not covered?"

"I'm Egyptian, not Saudi," my mother replied assertively. Foreign women were exempt from the requirement to wear an *abaya*—at least they were supposed to be—and we were Egyptian citizens.

With her soft, wavy, light-brown hair and green eyes, my mother hardly looked like a Saudi. Even at a distance, the *mutawwa* should have been able to see that we were foreigners, but apparently, he was too caught up in his self-righteousness to notice. "You are a Muslim woman, and you should dress like a Muslim woman!" he scolded. He spat out his comment as an order, not a suggestion.

My mother scowled at the man and kept walking. The *mutawwa* quickly crossed to our side of the street and began closing in. He positioned himself right in front of us, yelling at Mutti and gesturing menacingly with his whip. A crowd formed as he began lashing out at my mother's body, aiming for her bare arms and legs. I started screaming.

Mutti was having none of it. We may have been Egyptians but Mutti had a strong Teutonic streak in her. She didn't take orders well—actually, she didn't take orders at all—and certainly not from some stranger on a street corner.

The idea that this rude young man was trying to compel her to wear a shapeless black bag was absurd, and she dismissed it out of hand. "I am Egyptian," she repeated vehemently. "I've never worn an *abaya*, and I never will!" All the while, she kept her feet planted firmly onto the ground, even while deflecting his blows.

The *mutawwa's* face turned purple with rage. Brazen defiance from a woman was perhaps a new experience for him. When he raised his whip and attempted to flog her again, Mutti yanked it forcibly from his hands. Then she began to wield it against him, lashing him furiously about the shoulders, and cursing him all the while.

In an instant, several other *mutawwa* appeared and surrounded us. I tried to scream again, but this time no sound came out. I stood there in shock, afraid for what they would do to my mother. There was no more flogging, but Mutti and I were taken into custody and hauled off to a detention center. We sat there for several hours until they contacted my father and summoned him to come pick up his daughter and his unruly, "indecent" wife.

When he arrived at the jail to pick us up, Vati smoothed things over with tactful communication and his deliberately calm demeanor. He was the polar opposite of my mother. I often wondered in hindsight whether my father missed his calling as a diplomat.

I was still rattled and confused when we got safely home. I struggled to understand how it was possible that everyday clothing in Egypt could get you flogged in Saudi Arabia. As horrified as I was that my mother had barely escaped being whipped in public, I was also extremely proud of how she stood up to this bully. Vati was proud of her as well, and he assured her that he completely supported her position. Mutti continued to dress as she had in Cairo. And the *mutawwa* kept their distance and generally left us alone.

Though not nearly as lax as Egypt had been, Saudi Arabia was much more lenient from 1957 to 1960 than it is now regarding proper dress for women. Because of the relatively recent growth of fundamentalism and *wahabbism*, a strictly conservative form of Sunni Islam primarily practiced in Saudi Arabia, I doubt my mother would have gotten off so easily if the same thing had happened today.

In 1957, Saudi Arabia was considerably less developed than it is today. Oil production was in its earliest phases and the kingdom was not yet wealthy. The country as a whole struck me as a huge, barren desert—a vast expanse of sand punctuated by scattered towns and cities. Buildings in these communities were clustered together. They were fairly rudimentary, and most were made of pinkish mud or clay. In the smallest urban areas, street traffic was always congested. Cars and trucks moved chaotically—the noisy chorus of honking horns was constant. What was missing was anything green. Nothing resembled Cairo. In my little girl's mind, it all looked bleak and forbidding. The whole landscape made me anxious about what lay ahead.

Soon after our arrival in Saudi Arabia, we met Vati's longtime friend, Ahmed Zaki Yamani. They had studied law together at Cairo University. In the years since, Mr. Yamani had become the legal advisor to the oil and tax departments of the Saudi Ministry of Finance. After a heartfelt welcome to my parents, Mr. Yamani, a soft-spoken, mellow, and reserved gentleman with a black moustache and shortly trimmed beard, turned his attention to me and my brothers. At the time, there were three of us: Me, Tarek, who was 18 months my senior, and our younger brother Hazem, a toddler. Mr. Yamani's warmth and sincerity made us feel a bit more at ease in this unfamiliar new place.

Vati became Mr. Yamani's assistant, translating documents from Arabic into English. This was Vati's first paying job in Saudi Arabia, but the truth was that Mr. Yamani didn't really need Vati's help to translate anything: He had spent several years in the United States to further his studies, earning graduate degrees from both NYU and Harvard. He created a position specifically for Vati to give him a source of income. Vati knew it was a "make-work job," but he appreciated the opportunity to earn a modest living.

After a few months of Vati's "translating experience," we moved to Dhahran, a port city on the Persian Gulf. Notable for its massive oil reserves, Dhahran is home to Aramco, the giant oil company. It's now owned by the Saudi Arabian government, but when we were there, it was run by a consortium of American petrochemical corporations, including Texaco, Mobil, and Standard Oil. In Dhahran, Vati was able to secure a better position, translating documents for Aramco and for the Saudi government. Mr. Yamani was instrumental in making this new job opportunity possible too.

I still remember the air in Dhahran, which had a distinct, unpleasant odor. When I asked Vati what that pungent smell was, he told me it was the odor of petroleum. He went on to explain that

Saudi Arabia was in the process of drilling, extracting, and refining oil. "Lots of oil!" he exclaimed as he pointed to the multitudes of pumping machines bobbing up and down. They looked like donkeys at a watering hole. Day or night, they never stopped. And they were everywhere.

I saw a lot of poverty wherever we went. The beggars on the streets are forever etched in my mind. The majority of them were women completely covered in their black *abaya*. They looked like black boulders, squatting there. All I saw was their eyes as they watched for any gesture of someone handing them food or money. Many had their children with them, who were begging as well.

I was also saddened to see a number of people with only one hand. My parents explained that this was a result of punishment given to people who were caught stealing. First offense, one hand is chopped. Second offense, the other hand gets whacked. Other crimes were punishable by anything from public flogging to the death sentence.

The overall crime rate in Dhahran was low but public beheadings seemed to take place on a regular basis in the town square. Townspeople were invited and encouraged to witness this gruesome administration of justice. Fortunately, my parents never attended any of these events. Because we were young, they never talked to us about these horrific things unless we asked. My parents emphasized that although they didn't agree with Saudi Arabia's harsh punishment for breaking the law, they were in no position to make any comment about it.

For as long as I can remember, I have always questioned everything. If my questions weren't answered or didn't make sense to me, it would invariably frustrate or upset me. Vati saw my inquisitiveness as something to be celebrated, not punished. "At any and every given moment in one's life, there's an opportunity to learn or to teach," he would tell me. "Sometimes even both at the same time. We learn through experience, whether it's our own or another's, and we teach by example, by how we live our lives."

He knew that my questioning sprang from curiosity, not defiance, but my mother never seemed to appreciate the distinction. Mutti was the antithesis of my father. She expected blind obedience and didn't believe that children should question their parents' decisions. She often told me that I had resisted her from the moment of my birth. She saw my temperament as nothing more than insubordination, and insubordination always had consequences. I seemed to always be punished. "But why?" I frequently asked her. Rather than explaining to me what I wanted to know, her reply often was just one terse word: "Because!"

My mother seldom allowed herself to express love or adoration towards me. It wasn't a question of her inability to express love, because she was able to express it to my father and my brothers. From a very early age, I felt that I was treated differently and was not equal to the rest of my family in my mother's eyes.

As we began settling into our new lives in Dhahran, it soon became apparent that education was going to be a problem, specifically *my* education. Among the general Saudi population, education for girls was simply nonexistent. Children of foreigners attended special English language schools, but since we didn't know English, this didn't seem like a viable solution.

Vati expressed his concern to Mr. Yamani, who by this time was the legal adviser to the Saudi Council of Ministers, which included the future king, Crown Prince Faisal. Mr. Yamani had the ear of the young prince, who was very proactive about education for girls. The Crown Prince gave his permission for me to enroll in the royal *madrassa*, or school, for daughters of the royal family. My brother, Tarek, attended the boys' section of the royal *madrassa*.

The girls' *madrassa* had only one classroom, and it was very basic. Our desks resembled old-fashioned picnic tables. Three or four girls sat on long wooden benches at a shared table, facing the blackboard. There were always two teachers in the classroom. One gave the lesson of the day, writing on the board while talking to us—which meant that her back was to the room. The other teacher kept her eye on the students, watching for mischief and making sure we were paying attention. Talking or giggling was prohibited and punished just as it had been for centuries: Rulebreakers had to stay after school and write on the chalkboard, over and over, what they shouldn't have done. I remember writing, "I will not talk with my friends in the classroom" again and again, probably 50 times. It took a long time, and my hand hurt long before I was finished, but it helped me practice writing in Arabic.

I had learned to speak Arabic in Egypt, but now I was learning to read and write it as well. In Cairo, Tarek and I had been taught in German and French at the German Protestant Elementary School we attended. Although Muslim and fluent in Arabic, now in Saudi Arabia, Mutti was *also* determined that Tarek and I not lose our German language proficiency. Each day after school, she taught us basic German conversation and grammar. To polish our writing skills, we were given "homework" in the form of writing weekly letters to our German relatives. We lost touch with my father's relatives, and for reasons unknown to me, Vati never spoke about them.

But all lessons at the *madrassa* were given in Arabic. Speaking the language was very different from reading and writing it. Arabic, a Semitic language like Aramaic and Hebrew, has a completely different alphabet—and unlike Western languages, it is written from right to left.

I liked the other students. The girls were friendly and playful and got along well. That made sense since they were all related to each other. I was the odd one out, but I made friends right away.

We all dressed in the school uniform—a black, below-the-knee pleated cotton skirt, a white, short-sleeved cotton blouse, and white socks with black shoes. We wore our hair the same way too. Each of us had long, brown hair neatly corralled into either a ponytail or braids. Our teachers—all women, to be sure—wore the same uniform. Whenever they went outdoors, however, they donned the traditional *abaya* over their clothing.

On the first day of school, I already had a problem. I raised my hand and waited patiently for the teacher to call my name. Too shy to speak up, I jumped up and ran to her, then I whispered in her ear, "May I please use the toilet?"

"Of course," she replied with a warm smile. She then called on another girl to take my hand and lead me to the restroom, which was located in another small building across from our classroom. As we approached the structure, an overwhelming stench wafted toward us. The other girl seemed oblivious to the odor as she led me into the building that housed the toilets.

Except that there were no toilets. There were only holes in the floor.

I noticed that the girl who had escorted me returned to the classroom, leaving me alone. I was bewildered. This was a school for the princesses of Saudi Arabia, and this was their bathroom? I knew that plumbing existed here, since our apartment had a kitchen with hot and cold running water and a modern bathroom with a regular toilet that flushed, just like we had in Cairo.

I stood there, frozen and perplexed, because I didn't know what to do. I was afraid that some creature might crawl out of the hole, up my leg, and into my bottom. I was even more afraid that I might lose my balance or that my foot would slip and I'd fall through the hole into the abyss of foul-smelling ooze below. I didn't pee until I got home.

The next day, sensing my confusion, my teacher explained to me how to maneuver the use of the "toilet" without falling in. She explained how to place my feet on each side of the opening before squatting down. She also reassured me that nothing would jump out at me from the hole.

In August 1957, my third brother, Sherief, was born. Because of Mr. Yamani and other acquaintances with connections to Aramco, Vati was able to arrange for Mutti to deliver Sherief at the Aramco hospital, which was Saudi Arabia's most modern medical facility. This was a potentially life-saving arrangement since other Saudi hospitals were quite primitive. Although initially disappointed to have yet another brother, Sherief was cute. He seemed so little, and I quickly overcame my disappointment to help Mutti with his care.

A THIRD GRADE SENIOR

In 1959, I entered third grade at the *madrassa*. In terms of education in Saudi Arabia, I was a high school senior: third grade was the highest level of education offered to the daughters of royalty.

Neither of my parents found this acceptable. The question was what to do about it. As he often did, Vati read the Qur'an, Hadiths, and Sunnahs, (recordings and detailed explanation of the words and deeds of Prophet Muhammed) and he prayed steadily to clarify his thinking. When he realized that the solution would mean leaving Saudi Arabia, my parents applied for permission to emigrate to the United States.

They were denied. In 1960, the US still had immigration quotas based on nationality, and the quota for North Africans was full. But my grandmother's determination to give birth to each of her children in Germany paid off: Mutti applied separately for permission to enter the United States. Because she held both German and Egyptian citizenship and the American system at the time was heavily weighted in favor of Western Europeans, her application was approved. Vati, my brothers, and I were permitted to accompany her as her immediate family members.

On the way to the United States, we stopped in Zurich to visit Tante Aidi, my mother's sister. The three weeks we spent there were uplifting for all of us. Tante Aidi was a physician. After a divorce, she'd moved to Zurich and started her life over. Now she lived in a spacious apartment with a beautiful view of the Alps. I felt an immediate bond with her. Her warm and loving presence reminded me so much of my grandmother. I loved how open-minded, independent, and progressive she was—she was the kind of woman I wanted to become. I vowed I would always find a way to keep her in my life. Tante Aidi was living proof that reinvention was not only possible but also energizing and life-changing.

My parents and I shared the same mix of excitement and trepidation over our move. When Vati sat alone during quiet moments, there was sorrow in his eyes, and I could almost feel the weight of worry on his heart. My parents were preparing to build a new life in a new country where they knew no one. We were arriving with no safety net, and Vati had no job prospects—there would be no one like Mr. Yamani to help us get settled. It was a tremendous risk, but through it all, my parents never lost their faith. They each continued to pray five times a day and they encouraged me and Tarek to do the same.

I knew nothing about the strange land called America other than that it had fought against the Germans in World War II. What would America look like? Where would I go to school? How would I make friends? How would I learn English?

Leaving Saudi Arabia for the United States was a pivotal point in my life, and it was due entirely to Vati's determination that

I had to have a good education. He was adamant in his belief that women, like men, should be independent, and he knew that education was the crucial first step toward independence.

It didn't quite go completely as planned.

CHAPTER 2

WELCOME TO AMERICA

Our first day in the United States is burned into my memory. We landed in New York from Switzerland on a hot and humid summer day.

Even though my education was the reason for our arrival, this was a new beginning for all of us. Our new home—the melting pot of nations—granted us freedom from the mortal danger that surely awaited us if we ever returned to Egypt. It also gave us the freedom to create the life my parents had envisioned—one that would allow us to prosper in a peaceful environment and earn a comfortable living, all while maintaining our cultural and religious values.

My father summoned two taxis, one for the six of us and one for our luggage. He asked that the drivers take us and our belongings to the closest hotel from the airport.

I remember seeing the drivers smiling at each other and wondering what they were thinking.

Our cabbie drove for what seemed like hours. Smushed in the back between Mutti and my three brothers, I was sweating from the heat and humidity, and my skin stuck to the vinyl seat because I was wearing a skirt.

My parents exchanged worried glances—the trip was taking much longer than it should have and the landmarks seemed to be the same every few minutes. "Where are you taking us?" my father politely asked, after realizing the drivers were cruising in circles, running up the fare. The cabbie didn't respond. He finally pulled up in front of a tall, drab building and motioned for us to get out. The second cab with our luggage was right behind us. The drivers deposited everything on to the sidewalk. They swiftly drove off after Vati paid them.

When we entered, I saw that it was a hotel, but it was filthy and full of cockroaches. Welcome to New York! I wondered how, in the city that was supposedly America's largest and most famous, we ended up in such a dump.

We all stayed in one room that night, which made the space feel warmer. I felt comforted knowing we were all together, but the room was so hot and I just *knew* cockroaches were on their way to get me.

I stared out the window, uncomfortable and anxious, with Tarek next to me. What had we gotten ourselves into?

Although the long journey from Switzerland had left me feeling tired, I spent a good amount of time checking out my surroundings and looking out the open window. My first thought was how quiet New York City seemed compared to Dhahran. The moving traffic yielded little noise compared to the sounds of the bustling streets of Dhahran. In Dhahran, there was no such thing as driving lanes, traffic lights, or even stop signs. People just seemed to drive in whatever random direction they chose, honking their horns through the traffic until they arrived at their destinations. Here, the traffic was orderly. It was so quiet that I could hardly believe New York was a much bigger city than Dhahran.

As I sat hovering at the window in silence, pondering the traffic with Tarek, I suddenly became aware of beautiful explosions of color in the sky. Tarek and I looked at each other, bemused. What were these streams of color, bursting open into the night with a crackling sound? I had never seen such a spectacular sight. My father explained that they were fireworks. I looked out the window again, and they were everywhere. But why? Tarek and I wondered if the city of New York was celebrating our family's arrival to the United States with fireworks!

Though it wasn't long before we learned the true reason for the fireworks, we relished the thought that a country would be so welcoming to us. I went to bed that night feeling happy and at peace. My father had mentioned something called the "American Dream." Now, around Independence Day, 1960, we found ourselves among the newest American immigrants in pursuit of the same dream. I didn't yet know what Vati meant by the "American Dream," but he said that in America, people are free to pursue and achieve anything they want. My father made it sound so simple. Little did we know just how difficult it would be to find our place in this new land and achieve our own American dreams.

We stayed in New York for one night. My parents were enchanted with California, specifically Los Angeles. They had learned about the "City of Angels" through friends and acquaintances, and they had heard of and seen movies produced out of Hollywood.

My parents opted to travel across the country by rail, allowing us to take in the breathtaking scenery along the way. The large billboards and signs were a novelty to me and Tarek. Of course, since we knew no English, we didn't understand the meanings of any of the advertisements or traffic signs, but we made a game out of trying to guess what they said. My favorite was the one with the little girl with yellow pigtails walking along the beach while a little black dog pulled on her panties. I wondered why the dog was biting her. I had no idea that it was an ad for Coppertone and that her panties were a swimsuit or that the dog wasn't biting, rather exposing her tan lines.

After several days' travel, we finally arrived on the West Coast.

LOS ANGELES AND THE SEGREGATED 1960S

In Los Angeles, the stifling humidity of New York was replaced by hotter, drier air, laced with a heavy dose of orange-brown smog. Vati found us a house in a middle-class neighborhood in Inglewood, not far from Los Angeles International Airport. It was pleasant, clean, and modestly furnished with a table, chairs, sofa, beds, and other essential items. We had everything we needed but there were no frills. Appliances like washing machines, clothes dryers, and televisions were still expensive at the time so they weren't included. We washed our clothes by hand and entertained ourselves with games, books, and family outings. But we had more than enough to occupy ourselves.

The 1960s were a turbulent time in the United States. Racial tensions were on everyone's mind and progress towards equity was uneven. Even though we were new immigrants, we immediately sensed the national mood, and it had a direct effect on my family. We couldn't help but stick out in our white, segregated neighborhood. Nobody else was Muslim or spoke Arabic. At a time when race was a hot topic, people didn't know what to make of us: We weren't black, but we weren't exactly white either. We were light brown, but we weren't Latinos. And we sure weren't Chinese or Japanese. Out of fear and ignorance, people were often rude or hostile to us.

FIRST DAY OF SCHOOL

In September 1960, Tarek and I started classes at our new American school. He was in fifth grade and I was in fourth. Hazem, age five, was enrolled in half-day kindergarten. Sherief, only three, stayed home with Mutti. The first day of school was a strange experience. We didn't know what to expect, but like all children at this age, I wanted to fit in and be accepted. Since I had never had a problem making friends, I hoped that I would meet them sooner rather than later. My naïve understanding of the state of the world in early 1960s would soon be shattered.

Teachers and classmates gathered around me and Tarek, talking at us in a language we couldn't understand. Knowing no English gave me an odd feeling of being alone. I remember randomly nodding my head "yes" or shaking it "no," simply to appear as though I understood something, even though I had no idea what anyone was saying.

I soon learned that the easiest way for me to learn English was phonetically, just as I had learned German in Cairo. It certainly helped that I was familiar with the Latin alphabet, although unlike German, in which every word is spoken as it is written, English presented great challenges in pronunciation. Words like "people" and "enough" were especially difficult. And English grammar seemed to have more exceptions than rules, a stark contrast to the rigid German grammar structure that I had learned.

I remember meticulously spelling out the letters of each new English word I learned so that I could associate them with their respective sounds.

Tragedy Hits Our Family

"Nixon or Kennedy?" my classmate to my right asked me, looking at me expectantly, her eyebrows raised. My English was still rudimentary, so I stared back at her and smiled, grateful for this friendly interaction that had interrupted my reverie. I'd been deep in thought, mourning the recent tragic death of my dear Onkel Rolf. Only a few days earlier, we had received a telegram from

Tante Aidi in Switzerland. Mutti and Aidi's brother was dead. The plane he was flying for *Misr-Air* (Egypt Air) had crashed off the coast of Sicily. There were no survivors.

We were devastated. Onkel Rolf had arranged our flights when we escaped to Saudi Arabia. His children were about the age of me and my brothers. I remember crying endlessly, thinking about my cousins in Cairo and what they were going through. My heart ached for my grandmother as well. She'd already been rocked by grief and loss; while we were in Dhahran my grandfather had suffered a stroke and died. And now her son had been suddenly taken from her.

The worst of it was that there was little we could do to comfort her. We couldn't travel to Egypt because Vati was still wanted for treason. As long as Nasser was in power, my father would be captured and executed if he returned. And we weren't sure what would happen to the rest of us.

The only thing my parents could do was reach out by phone. I remember hearing them struggle with an overseas operator, trying to explain that they needed her assistance in placing a call to Cairo. Years later, I learned that the operator kept repeating to them that it would take time to set it up, and she had a hard time making them understand that they had to hang up while she did that. When she finally called back, she had my grandmother on the line. Mutti and Vati were both crying as they spoke with her. Because overseas calls were so expensive, the call was brief. My parents followed up with regular telegrams and letters to my grandmother. Tarek and I wrote weekly letters to her, as well as to my cousins. My parents enclosed them along with their own letters to comfort them.

Shortly after Onkel Rolf's passing, Mutti learned she was pregnant. At first, it was hard for her to find joy in this new pregnancy, but as time passed, she used the preparations for the arrival of her fifth child as a distraction from the grief of losing her brother. I dealt with the sadness of Onkel Rolf's death by concentrating on learning English and trying to make new friends.

"So Nixon or Kennedy?" my classmate asked again.

I had heard those words before, but I wasn't sure what they meant. I asked Vati about it that evening, and he explained that the Americans were in the process of choosing a new president, and that Richard M. Nixon and John F. Kennedy were the names of the two candidates.

The idea that citizens of a country voted for their leaders was utterly strange to me. I didn't understand much about the concept of democracy, mostly because I'd never lived in one before. President Nasser had taken over Egypt in a coup and then placed Egypt's first president under house arrest, and Saudi Arabia was a monarchy. Nevertheless, I was most interested in democracy and eager to learn. I tried to pick up as much information as I could.

Following politics and the news turned out to be a great way to improve my English. Storefronts often had TVs in them back then, and sometimes I was able to catch glimpses of the candidates making speeches as I walked by. My parents learned along with me. Even though they couldn't vote in the election, they followed the presidential race as closely as they could.

All of us came to prefer Kennedy. He struck me as having a kind heart and an empathetic soul. I was happy when he won.

Without having much knowledge of English, I kept to myself. And being alone required no effort on my part because I was shunned. Tarek was too. We were the darkest children in the school, and no one wanted anything to do with us. The other kids gawked at us and treated us as if we were strange and somehow unclean simply because our skin was brown.

One day, some children encircled me during recess and began mocking me. One of the girls pulled at my hair, while one of the boys tugged at my skirt and pulled it up to expose my panties. At other times, they just pointed at me and laughed. It was awful, and I struggled to make sense of how I was treated. I was the same girl who had no trouble making friends with princesses in Saudi Arabia, but here in the United States, I was an outcast. Did the color of my skin matter all that much?

Do I Actually Have a Friend?

In spite of the ridicule, I managed to find a friend. Her name was Bonnie Collins. Over the course of several weeks, she had tried to grab my attention in various ways by sitting next to me in class, showing me how to number the pages in my notebook, and eating lunch with me in the cafeteria. Although Bonnie and I couldn't understand each other very well, I knew she was reaching out to me and wanted to be my friend.

At recess during one of our playful exchanges that combined my broken English with animated body language, I somehow conveyed to Bonnie that my mother was expecting a baby. There on the playground, I tried to explain to Bonnie that I was worried about my mother because she didn't feel well and didn't have a doctor to care for her or the baby growing inside her.

Not long after that conversation, Bonnie invited me to her birthday party, which was a pool party and cookout. Mutti came with me, while Vati stayed home to look after my brothers. Several other kids from school were there and we had such fun together. It was the first time I felt accepted, like a normal kid at play. Although Mutti knew very little English, she sat at a table visiting with Bonnie's mother and some of the other parents, while I was having the time of my life in the swimming pool.

Bonnie's father arrived home shortly after the party started and introduced himself to Mutti. Later that night, I overheard my parents talking in the kitchen. Mutti was explaining that Bonnie's father was an obstetrician and that he had offered to take care of Mutti throughout the remainder of her pregnancy, including the delivery of her baby, without charge.

I saw this as a huge blessing and a great relief. We had no extended family, no other support network. Vati didn't have a job yet, so we didn't have any health insurance and money was tight. We were living on the savings my parents had brought with them. There was no way they would have been able to afford prenatal care.

My parents weren't accustomed to accepting charity and didn't feel comfortable having the doctor provide his services for free. Whenever he saw Mutti, they insisted on paying him in cash. Eventually, Mutti stopped going to see him—we had so little money that my parents couldn't pay him anymore, but they were too embarrassed to say so.

The Collins family gave me hope that there were other kind and compassionate people out there. One day, a group of cheerful teenage girls came to our door bearing gifts of household items and groceries. They were from the Young Women's Christian Association (YWCA), and they referred to themselves as the Y-Teens. They reached out to my family as part of their community social project since we were considered a family in great need.

I turned nine right after election day, and the Y-Teens brought me a new dress on my birthday. I loved its red velvet bodice and checkered black-and-white taffeta skirt. The Y-Teens also gave me a doll that I adored. Her name was Betsy Wetsy. To my surprise, when I "fed" the doll a bottle of water, her diaper got wet and she needed changing. I immediately clung to Betsy Wetsy and took care of her as if she were my own baby sister.

The Y-Teens introduced Thanksgiving to us, arriving at our home with a complete traditional feast. The kindness of the Y-Teens was in stark contrast to the way I was treated at school.

A New Baby, but Denied Care

When Mutti's contractions began, Vati drove her to the emergency room at Cedars of Lebanon Hospital, which is now called Cedars Sinai Medical Center. The hospital was nearby, and my father took some sense of comfort from its name. Once they arrived, Vati anxiously began to explain that Mutti was in labor with her fifth baby and that the contractions were frequent.

They were turned away. Even as Mutti was groaning in active labor, an emergency room staff member told my parents that because they had no medical insurance and not enough cash they had to leave immediately.

Desperate and not knowing what to do, Vati called Dr. Collins. He instructed Vati to drive to a different hospital and promised that he would meet them there. On March 6, 1961, at Daniel Freeman Hospital in Inglewood, Mutti gave birth to another son. *Will I ever have a sister?* I thought, feeling sorry for myself. Having brother number four surely was another disappointment for me, but when Mutti brought him home, my heart just melted. He was adorable. Mutti named him Rolf after her late brother, but we decided to call him "Ralph."

In the spring of 1961, my parents were so low on money that making the rent was starting to be a problem. With five kids to support and Vati still out of work, we had to move to a more modest home in a working-class neighborhood.

I lost Bonnie, my only friend.

LENNOX, CALIFORNIA

Once again, my family stood out: we were foreign, we didn't speak English well, and we were darker than everyone else in our neighborhood.

We moved to an area called Lennox, just south of Inglewood but part of a different school district. With only a few months left in the school year before I completed fourth grade, I was "the new kid" once more.

Again, I became a target for taunting and ridicule. Kids would come up to me and shout something, then laugh and run away. At first, it didn't bother me because I couldn't understand them. Thinking it was a game, I laughed with them and shouted back in my best English, not knowing what I was saying.

There was one other girl in my class with really dark skin, even darker than mine. Her name was Carla. One day, I saw her sitting by herself during recess, crying. I walked over to her, sat down beside her, and placed my arm over her shoulders. I could feel that she was hurting, but I didn't understand why. I only knew that the same kids who shouted at me had done the same to her, and whatever they said had upset her.

Soon enough, my ignorance no longer protected me from the taunts of my classmates, and I was able to understand what they were saying. Words like harem dancer, camel rider, and Egyptian mummy were among the first words I learned. Then came phrases like "Hey little Egypt, show us some belly dances" or reciting the song "Ahab the Arab." It was cruel and hurtful and it continued with a vengeance, and as I began to comprehend the ugliness behind it, school became an unbearable place to be.

My father was my biggest source of comfort through all of this, but he was away most of the time, either working or looking for work. He took whatever jobs he could find, often two or three at once. In his home country, Vati was at the top of his field, but in America, he was a bread deliveryman, a security guard, a milkman, a photo re-toucher. He usually didn't return home until bedtime. He looked drained and weary, but as exhausted as he was, he was never too tired to spend time with his "precious children," as he called us.

Tarek and I fell into a weekday routine. Immediately upon coming home from school, we had a snack, usually a piece of fruit, then sat at the kitchen table to practice our English lessons and complete our homework. Mutti gave us our German lessons as she had in Saudi Arabia. When Vati came home, he reviewed our homework assignments.

After completing his homework, Tarek could do whatever he pleased. Not me. As the only girl, my job was to help my mother with the household chores. In both Cairo and Dhahran, Mutti always had domestic help, a woman who functioned as a combination cook/housekeeper/nanny. But now my parents could no longer afford help so we did everything ourselves.

Weekdays were busy enough, but on the weekends, my chores were endless. I became Cinderella, helping Mutti with the dusting, the vacuuming, the mopping, the cooking, and worst of all, the laundry. Since we had no washing machine, we washed everything by hand.

Every Saturday morning, we gathered all the family's dirty clothes into the bathtub, including my brothers' denim jeans, baby Ralph's cloth diapers, and all the towels and sheets. I carried the diapers, t-shirts, and white cotton underwear to the kitchen. We had a huge pot designated for laundry only. Mutti filled it with a solution of water, detergent, and bleach. Then she boiled the diapers and underwear for 10 minutes before taking them to the bathtub to scrub and rinse.

Washing clothes in the tub made my back ache, and scrubbing the laundry with my bare hands, knuckle to knuckle caused painful, bleeding cracks that opened up in my dry skin. Mutti didn't know about washboards since our domestic help washed our laundry before we came to America. When I hung the wash on the clothesline, I had to be extra careful not to get the blood from my hands onto the clean laundry.

That was not the end of my responsibilities. I also took care of my younger brothers, especially baby Ralph. I quickly learned how to prepare his formula, bottle-feed him, burp him, change his diaper, and bathe him. I also comforted and soothed him when he cried or needed something.

Then an angel from heaven was sent, but in her natural stoic manner, Mutti initially rejected her offers to help.

Leona to the Rescue

One afternoon, I was taking Ralph for one of our regular walks when I came upon a sturdy-looking woman of about 40. She had light brown, very curly, short hair, and she was working in her garden. Her tanned skin was proof that she spent a lot of time there.

I stopped as she looked at me. "Hi honey," she said.

I thought for a few seconds about how to respond with my newly learned English words. "Hi," I replied, adding with much pride, "I have a new baby brother. Isn't he cute?"

The woman looked at me in a sweet, motherly way after peering into the stroller to see Ralph. He was only three months old.

"I'm Leona. What's your name?"

Eventually, she met my brothers and my parents and, as she put it, "absolutely fell in love with our whole family." When I was much older, she admitted that she thought my father was the most handsome man she had ever met. She also felt a connection with Mutti and wondered how such a young woman who spoke limited English could fare with five small children and a husband who held down several part-time jobs.

Leona's husband, Ed, was a trucker and on the road a lot. Her loving, daily companions were two dachshunds: Hermie and his sister, Hilda. Leona was one of the first Americans I met who accepted us unconditionally.

And for me, a girl who was still searching for any kind of acceptance at school, that was everything. She didn't know what Islam was or anything about our heritage but she loved us anyway. She didn't care that we were broke or that we were brown. She also offered practical help and advice. She introduced my parents to food stamps now known as the federal nutritional assistance program (SNAP) and showed them how and where to apply.

When Ed was away, Leona invited us over—*all* of us. On Sunday evenings, she served us ice cream and sat down with us to watch *Bonanza* since she knew we didn't have a television. Leona loved us as a family, but she also had individual relationships with each of us kids.

As much as I loved going out to lunch with Leona or watching TV at her house, my most cherished times with her were spent in her garden. Leona grew her own vegetables each summer. When I showed interest, she offered to pay me 50 cents for each gardening task or to mow her small lawn. It wasn't the most glamorous work in the world, particularly with Leona's push reel mower, but it allowed me to spend some quality time outside and with Leona.

It made us both happy at the time and in the long run. It gave Leona great joy to pass on her gardening skills to me, and her delight became the seed that would eventually grow into my own love of gardening. Spending time with Leona was a welcome escape from my reality. She had an open ear, always listening to whatever I wanted to talk about, and an open heart for me. I felt so comfortable with her, just as I did with my grandmother.

Leona's love and kindness quelled many of the anxieties I felt at home, seeing as my relationship with Mutti wasn't any better. Leona came to our house on one of those dreaded Saturday mornings when Mutti and I were on our knees at the bathtub, scrubbing clothes by hand. Leona offered to let my mother use her washing machine. It was one of those old wringer styles with two rollers on top.

"Inge, for God's sake!" Leona said. "Look at Mona—that poor girl, workin' so hard and gettin' all sweaty! Why don't you bring your laundry over and use my washer?"

I lit up at the prospect of being liberated from the household chore I hated the most. I thought to myself, *Finally, thank goodness*. But my mother quickly shook her head. "She's all right. She's going to do the laundry because I said so," Mutti replied, glaring at me. It took all I had to fight back tears. Many years later, Leona shared with me how angry she was with my mother and how she had argued with her on many occasions in my defense concerning all the tasks I was responsible for and how poorly she treated me.

One evening, my father announced that we were moving again, this time to St. Louis, Missouri. Two years of financial hardship in Los Angeles had taken its toll. It was too difficult to make ends meet. My parents were told that the cost of living was more affordable in the Midwest, and an American Vati met in Saudi Arabia while translating for Aramco had promised him a job in St. Louis. Vati contacted him after realizing his minimum-wage jobs in Los Angeles were not sufficient enough to meet the family's financial needs. This person reassured Vati that he could assist him with a translating job in St. Louis if he wanted to relocate.

There were many reasons why I wasn't looking forward to the move, but the worst of it was losing contact with Leona. My grandmother and Tante Aidi were thousands of miles away across the Atlantic Ocean, and now I was moving away from the only other sympathetic adult female figure in my life.

CHAPTER 3

OH, NO! NOT AGAIN

The blustering wind and bitter cold made me shiver as we sat in the car. *What if we freeze to death?* I thought, as Vati got out to put chains on the tires.

It was the late fall of 1963. We had packed up all of our belongings once again. We loaded our few household items into a U-Haul trailer hitched to our car and set out onto Route 66. The weather turned nasty as we traveled east, and we drove headlong into a winter storm just outside of Albuquerque. This was my first snowstorm, and I was scared. So were my brothers. I didn't feel safe until we were tucked into a hotel room for the night.

SAINT LOUIS

Things were no better once we arrived in St. Louis. Vati had neither the friend nor the job he had been promised. When Vati reported to the office where he was supposed to work, he was told this person didn't work there and that no one had any knowledge of the position he'd been offered. Try as he might, Vati was unable to contact or track this man down. It was difficult for me, as a child, to understand how such a situation could have come about. My parents didn't talk about this humiliating experience with us kids, except to satisfy my constant questioning. As I grew older, I came to understand that my father took the man at his word as was customary in our culture. The emptiness in his eyes and solemn expression conveyed his regret in making this move, yet he remained upbeat and reassured us that everything would be okay.

My parents were in a quandary. It was as if we'd picked up and moved halfway across the country for nothing. Vati would have to find work somehow, but first my parents had to find us a place to live and enroll us in school. We stayed in a temporary, motel-like room we could rent by the week until my parents were able to find more suitable housing.

Our schoolmates in St. Louis were even crueler to us than the kids in Inglewood had been. Little did we know that we'd been enrolled in what had previously been an all-white school during the pre-civil rights era. There were no black or brown children in our school. Tarek and I were the darkest students.

Tarek was taunted, mocked, and bullied. It was the same for Sherief and Hazem. The boys picked on them and regularly called out insults like "desert rats," "dirty Arabs," or "desert niggers, go back to live in your tents where you belong." Two favorites were "Arab sucker" and "Egyptian germs." The former referred to our last name, Sakr, and the latter to our Egyptian/German heritage. On many occasions, I found myself in the midst of physical fights with the neighborhood boys as I tried to protect my little brothers.

Hazem was in third grade and Sherief was in first. Ralph, now two, was the only child still at home. Tarek and I were in junior high now: He was in the eighth grade and I was in the seventh. Or so I thought. Tarek was actually in the seventh grade, on a different schedule than mine. By this time, my English was pretty good, but Tarek's accent was thicker so he'd been kept back a grade.

Vati landed his first job in St. Louis as a milkman. It was full time and minimum wage but at least it was a job. *Alhamdulillah—*

"thanks be to God." Soon, we had a duplex apartment. Our new residence turned out to be a huge stroke of good fortune because Betty and Andy Johnson lived in the other half of the duplex. We met them the day we moved in. Their two children, Don and Shirley, were a couple of years older than me and Tarek and were already in high school.

Andy Johnson was an engineer the same age as my father. He was also incredibly kind. It was Mr. Johnson who helped Vati secure a second job as a security guard, but that meant we hardly ever saw him. He left early in the morning to deliver milk and didn't come back until late at night when his shift as a watchman was over. Most weekdays, we children were already in bed and fast asleep by the time he came home.

Betty Johnson was a few years older than Mutti. She considered herself a homemaker, although she volunteered a few hours a week at the local library. Every time I saw her, she was cheerful and neatly dressed. We had only one car, which Vati needed to go to work, so Mrs. Johnson drove Mutti around town showing her the supermarkets, drug stores, health department, library, and other important destinations. She helped Mutti apply for food stamps in St. Louis and got Tarek enrolled in the Boy Scouts, in the same troop as Don.

THE IMPACT OF A PRESIDENT

I was watching the kids in my class play dodgeball and tetherball during recess on a typical Friday afternoon. Sitting alone on the bench, I was captivated by their antics and exuberance, daydreaming of the day when I could join in on the fun. On the other side of the bench, teachers were talking to each other while pointing their index fingers to their heads. I had no idea what they were talking about or what that gesture meant until I got home and saw that Mutti had the television on. That wasn't unusual for her because she loved to watch soap operas. But this time, the news was on and Walter Cronkite was making an announcement.

President Kennedy had been shot in the head. He had been assassinated. What? Why? I was only 12, and I struggled to understand why anyone would want to kill this president whom I learned to love as I learned the English language.

Although I had doubts and anxieties during our turbulent first years in the US, I still felt that I had an equal chance to succeed because of President Kennedy's inspiring inauguration speech. Even though my English was still not very good, I had been moved by Kennedy's inauguration address, especially the part where he said, "Ask not what your country can do for you—ask what you can do for your country."

And this was my country now. I carried his words in my heart throughout my life and aspired to follow them. I dreamed of someday communicating with, or even meeting, a President of the United States. Of course, I was yet to learn about the different parties and the politics behind them. I would learn that not all presidents were like JFK.

In school I was eager to learn—more eager than my teachers were to teach me. I remember having to press them to answer my questions and explain things I didn't understand. One teacher walked around the room helping all of my classmates but not me. I repeatedly raised my hand to request help, but he always told me I needed to wait my turn. It never came.

Tarek and I were on our own when it came to doing homework and prepping for tests. The teachers ignored us, Mutti didn't know English well enough to help us, and Vati got home too late at night. Not surprisingly, our grades were not good. One of our school counselors informed my parents that Tarek and I probably wouldn't amount to anything more than menial workers *if* we completed school at all.

When my parents heard this, they were livid. I overheard them talking in their bedroom in Arabic. "*Mish maa uul*—unbelievable! How can they say such a thing?" Vati asked Mutti. "Our children know three languages and are learning a fourth! How can they say that?" This was one of my earliest memories of hearing outrage in my father's voice.

Between our skin color, our accents, and our Arabic surname, we stood out. Every day in the cafeteria, I got the message that I didn't belong there and would never be accepted. Day after day, I ate lunch alone because no one wanted to sit with me.

Mutti packed our lunches every day because we were Muslim and didn't eat pork, ham, or bacon—and the cafeteria menu was full of it. This was a time before beef or turkey hot dogs and lunch meats. Everything was made of pig meat. One of the most popular school lunch items was something they called "pigs in a blanket," a hot dog wrapped up in some kind of biscuit.

We had brown bread with cheese or meat that Mutti sliced from the previous night's leftovers for lunch. Often it was tuna or chicken, but our favorite lunchmeat was boiled cow's tongue. Every Friday, Vati bought them for a nominal price from a small neighborhood food market. The butcher saved them for him simply because no one else was going to buy them. In the cafeteria, the other students were already so disgusted that the bread I ate was brown and not white—I didn't dare tell them the meat was cow's tongue.

Then we were introduced to what we later learned was the "all-American sandwich." I clearly remember the day Vati brought home something I hadn't seen before. It was a glass jar filled with a light brown, creamy substance. I glanced at my brothers as we all sat around our small, round kitchen table and watched with anticipation as Vati opened the jar and scraped out a little bit with a butter knife.

I even dipped my finger into the jar as Vati explained that it was made from peanuts that had been ground until they became smooth and buttery. I loved the way its luscious, creamy taste melted slowly as I rolled my tongue around the roof of my mouth.

From then on, peanut butter was a daily treat for all of us. Although we had never heard of such a food before, we quickly learned how to make various peanut butter sandwiches with jelly, bananas, and honey. And they were so tasty. I thought bringing peanut butter and jelly sandwiches to lunch would help me fit in better, especially if I shared them. The all-American sandwich for the all-American kid, so to speak. It didn't make a difference though, as no one noticed and no one cared. Eventually, the teasing and shunning got worse—and it got physical.

One cold wintery day, the usual group of girls waited for me behind some bushes after school let out. They jumped on me, knocked my books out of my arms, and pulled me to the ground. Once they got me down, the girls pinned my limbs while a heavy girl sat on me. She punched me in the face as they chanted slurs like "Arab bitch" and "Muslim bitch."

Another group of kids formed a circle around us and stood there, cheering on my tormentors. After they were done hammering me, one of the girls told me she needed to "wash" my face because it was "too dark and dirty." She proceeded to rub my face with a mixture of snow and sand.

When the bullies had finally finished with me, everyone quickly scattered in different directions. I was left alone and aching, my face bloody and prickling with pain. I picked up my books and papers and ran home, crying and in shock.

Mutti was alarmed when she saw me. When Vati came home from work and found out what had happened, he was shaken as well. My parents accompanied me to school the next day and met with the principal once more. Despite seeing the scratches and bruises on my swollen face, he gave his standard aloof response. "We're not responsible for what happens after school and away from school grounds," he said. That was it.

I decided it was time to fight back.

One spring afternoon, I was walking home from school when I saw one of the girls who had beaten me. This time, she was alone. I hid behind a bush, and after checking to be sure no one else was watching, I jumped out and grabbed her. After wrestling her to the ground, I sat on her, pinning her wrists to the pavement with my knees, just as she had done to me.

My pain and anguish were fresh in my mind as I began punching and pounding her over and over again, the very same way she had punched me. "You bitch!" I yelled at her in my rage and fury. "Tell your bitch friends that I will do the same to them, one by one, and to you again if any of you bitches continue to tease me." The word "bitch" was new to my vocabulary—indeed, I had learned it from them. Before I let her get up off the ground, I yanked out a clump of her hair as a trophy, proof that I had finally defeated one of my bullies.

As I walked home with a fistful of blonde hair, I felt horror at what I had done. At the same time, I felt relief and satisfaction that I had gotten revenge. Mutti was speechless when I arrived, but after I explained what I'd done, she told me she was quite impressed. To this day, it remains one of the few times in my life when Mutti expressed a sense of pride in me as her daughter. Perhaps, she finally saw a little of herself in what I had done—she was, after all, the woman who had grabbed a whip out of the hands of a member of the Saudi religious police and started using it on him.

Later that night, I kept thinking about the incident. In a strange way, I felt remorse for beating up the girl. I wished I had a chance to tell her that I didn't really mean to hurt her. I wanted her to understand how much it hurt to be teased and beaten. I wanted to tell her I was sorry, but I never did.

Vati tried to comfort me when he came home that night. "It's not a good thing to fight," he said softly. "But sometimes we must defend ourselves as our Prophet Muhammed did when he was called upon to do so." He read the Hadith regarding this topic. Then he pulled out his Qur'an to read the verse pertaining to defense: "To those against whom transgression is made, permission is given to fight, because they are wronged and verily God is most powerful for their aid."

After the incident, the girls and all the other kids in school kept their distance from me and left me in peace.

But Vati couldn't bear to see us suffering. We were trying so hard to fit in with a society that let us know every day that we were not wanted because we were different. My parents reasoned that we might find more opportunities in Los Angeles and perhaps a little more acceptance this time around. Within a few months, we all headed back to the West Coast.

CHAPTER 4

INGLEWOOD II

When we arrived back in California, we moved into a modest house in the same Lennox/Inglewood neighborhood where we had lived before. It was humble but familiar. Vati landed a job not far away, albeit another minimum wage one. Best of all, Ed and Leona were nearby.

I went back to helping Leona in her garden, and whenever she needed extra help with special projects around the house, I jumped at the opportunity. I enjoyed being with Leona, and I loved the sense of independence and emotional support I got from being with her. Leona paid me the same 50 cents for each chore, and knowing I had a little money in my pocket—money I had earned myself—gave me an added sense of security.

THE FIRST STEP IN MY TRANSFORMATION

On my first day of ninth grade, I took out a sheet of paper to take notes in US history class and proudly wrote my new name in the top right-hand corner: Mona Johnson. My new name! I was exhilarated. Overjoyed. My family took a momentous step forward when we became US citizens—all of us except Ralph, who was already a citizen because he was born here. On September 10,

1965, the whole family went downtown to the Superior Court-house. Leona came with us as our character witness, attesting that we would be honorable citizens and would not pose any threat to the government or the people of the United States. In front of the judge, we raised our right hands and pledged the Oath of Allegiance that all new citizens take.

Finally, we were Americans, and one of the perks of citizenship was that we would now be permitted to change our names. Wanting to blend in seamlessly into American society, Vati immediately took advantage of this opportunity—we all got new American names to go with our new American citizenship. He changed our last name to Johnson in honor of Betty and Andy Johnson, our kind and supportive neighbors in St. Louis. (To this day, the memory of our year and a half in St. Louis conjures up intensely sad feelings. The Johnsons were the *only* people in St. Louis who showed us any love and compassion. Their open-mindedness and grace in accepting and respecting our family is forever imprinted in my heart, and I am proud my father chose their name for us to carry.)

My father's full name became Richard Allen Johnson. Tarek dropped the first syllable of his name to become Rick. Hazem chose John after his favorite movie star, John Wayne, and Sherief became Jerry, the Americanized version of Sherry, which was already his nickname. Mutti kept her first name, Inge, and I was now Mona Johnson. At first, it felt weird to suddenly have a new identity, but it didn't take long to get used to it.

We enrolled in new and different schools as the Johnson kids. This made a huge difference. By now, my brothers and I all spoke unaccented English. We didn't have to explain ourselves or tell anyone where we came from. Life in high school as Mona Johnson, a freshman, was a lot easier than life as Mona Gulinar Sakr in middle school.

Being a new ninth grader named Johnson made me very happy: I had ended eighth grade with a humiliating disaster. I had three friends who were Mexican-American girls. They told me about the tradition of passing around autograph books at the end of the school year. These were mementos in the making so we could remember our classmates as they progressed into high school and later in life. I bought myself one and circulated it to my classmates. It disappeared for several hours, and I had no idea where it was until my teacher handed it to me at the end of the day. I walked home, anxiously anticipating what I would read in it.

It was devastating. Most of the entries were insults to my nationality, skin color, and religion. Some students wrote "to the desert rat," "to the dirty Arab," "to the desert nigger," and so on.

One contemptuous student was especially hateful: *Roses are red. Arabs are black. If I had a knife, I'd stab you in the back.*

I tore the autograph book into thousands of pieces and threw it away. When I told my mother what happened, she shrugged it off and told me I was being too sensitive. I desperately needed comfort from Mutti, which I didn't get, and I cried the rest of the day and into the night.

I wanted to talk to Vati about it, but his work schedule prevented us from seeing each other. When I finally saw him days later, he consoled me with his usual optimism. "This too shall pass, my dear daughter," he said, quoting from an ancient Sufi parable. My father wanted me to view this as another obstacle to overcome and to see how dealing with it would make me more resilient for the future. He was basically telling me the same thing as Mutti had but in a softer way. Mutti was more blunt, to the point, and matter of fact, and I was too sensitive for that response.

In high school, my after-school routine didn't change. I did my homework and completed German lessons Mutti had prepared. Gradually, Tarek and I lost our French because we had no one to practice with. Both parents wanted us to retain our Arabic as well. This made us a trilingual household. Our conversations with Mutti were all in German, and we spoke to Vati in English and Arabic. My brothers and I spoke a mixture of all three languages to one another.

Tarek joined another Boy Scout troop and became friends with Oscar Guerrero, who was Mexican-American, and our families became good friends.

Oscar's mother, Mary, was much like Leona in that she was loving and maternal. She was always well-dressed and wore high heels everywhere she went. Her jet-black hair was nicely coiffed, and I don't think I ever saw her without makeup. She looked like a movie star.

Mrs. Guerrero always made herself available whenever I came to her house just to talk. They lived within walking distance in Hawthorne, the next town over. She listened to what I had to say, valued my opinion, and wanted to know what kinds of books and music I liked. She made me feel very special. I didn't feel special at home, and the majority of my conversations with Mrs. Guerrero were about my troubles with Mutti—why I didn't feel the affection from my own mother that I could see other mothers give their daughters and why I felt so distanced from her.

* * * * *

We'd finally bought a television, and my parents' favorite program was *The Lawrence Welk Show*. His variety show, with its Big Band overtones, was considered square even at its prime. I preferred the hipper music of the Beatles and the Beach Boys, not that my parents would ever let me attend one of their concerts.

However, they did get tickets to *The Lawrence Welk Show*, and I was the only one who got to go with them. I enjoyed Welk's old-fashioned music more than I thought I would, but I was still happy no one I knew could see me in the audience. As I sat there thinking that my anonymity was intact, I heard an announcement that the evening was a special occasion for a 13-year-old named Mona. I looked around the room, wondering if perhaps I had misunderstood or—as unlikely as it seemed—whether the announcement was in recognition of someone else with the same name as me.

The next moments were a bit of a blur—within seconds, Lawrence Welk whisked me across the dance floor as my parents looked on. They somehow made this happen. After all of my upsetting experiences, they wanted me to have a special moment. Of course, I was horrified at first. *What if someone from school saw me?* I thought. I didn't want to be labeled as a "square."

But as Mr. Welk spun me around the dance floor as the music played and the audience clapped, I felt like a princess! That night became one of the most memorable of my life.

* * * * *

Just as I started feeling less different at school, I got my period. I had no idea what this natural biological process would do to my life. In terms of my intellectual development, my parents were progressives. Culturally, however, they were still from the Old World, and they were extremely conservative in their beliefs about how teenage girls ought to behave. They never fully made peace with modern Western culture, and the fact that teen music, dress, and behavior were becoming increasingly permissive only heightened their belief that I had to be shielded from negative influences. As soon as my womanhood began, it was essential to them that I be kept away from the opposite sex.

Most of the time, when I wasn't in school, I pretty much had to stay home. I was either doing my homework, listening to music on the radio, or reading. I was especially interested in the American frontier and legendary figures like Buffalo Bill, Jesse James, Wild Bill Hickok, and Wyatt Earp. While my brothers filled their free time with hobbies, baseball, and scouting, I still had to help Mutti with the many household chores that needed to be done—and with four brothers, the chores were endless.

I felt like a prisoner in my own home. I wasn't allowed to go to friends' houses to visit, although my friends could visit me. Sleepovers were forbidden. I wasn't allowed to socialize with boys and dating was out of the question. "Whenever an unrelated or unmarried man and woman are alone, there's always a third presence: *alshaytan* [Satan]" was a mantra I often heard as a teen. These rules didn't apply to any of my brothers, even though I was raised to believe that I was their intellectual equal. I deeply resented the double standard.

On a positive note, when the Bolshoi ballet came to perform at the Hollywood Bowl, my parents took me; they knew I would love it and could see that I was struggling with the limitations on my personal freedoms. But even this fleeting evening of fun couldn't replace having a normal American teenage life.

Despite the cover of my new American name, I was still reserved at Morningside High. I was afraid of getting my feelings hurt again, but that was only part of the reason I kept to myself. Even if I made friends, my parents wouldn't let me go out with them. I wanted to be a cheerleader but that was forbidden. And I was barred from any after-school activities unless I was chaperoned by my big brother, Rick. And he, of course, was busy with his own friends and his own life.

One of my closest friends was a Mexican-American girl named Annette. Annette was a happy, free-spirited girl, and I connected with her from the moment we met. Whenever I admired her clothes, she would tell me how her mother would shop for fabric scraps and then stay up all night to sew her a new outfit. I often imagined how wonderful it would be to have a mom like that, a mom who spent so much time and effort providing happiness for her daughter.

Annette liked to go out on Friday and Saturday nights to listen to music. The Sunset Strip was lined with clubs like the Roxy, the Whisky-a-Go-Go, Gazzari's, and the Troubadour. Annette asked me if I wanted to go with her to see the Turtles and Three Dog Night. That, of course, was absolutely out of the question as far as my parents were concerned.

It's not that I didn't fight back—I tried, but whenever I questioned why I was being treated this way, I paid the price. My mother was the enforcer, and her role as my "warden" worsened our already rocky relationship. Mutti still expected blind obedience from me, exactly as she had when I was a toddler.

I never understood why my mother was so cold and distant. Tante Aidi, Mutti's sister, was warm and kind, and when we were still in Cairo, their mother, my grandmother, had always provided a loving counterpoint to Mutti's harshness. My relationships with Leona and with Mrs. Guerrero gave me the kind of warm comfort my own mother couldn't, or wouldn't, provide.

"I'm so glad I only have one daughter," I overheard Mutti say to Leona one day when she came to visit us. I was stung by the remark—it was as if I'd been slapped in the face. All I could do was tiptoe into the bathroom where I wept silently. Her cruel comment haunted me and added to what I felt was mounting proof that my mother didn't love me.

Over the years, I wondered what caused my mother to not want another daughter. It wasn't until decades later that I came to understand that it was a manifestation of my mother's personality coupled with the traditional cultural beliefs my parents valued: The utmost importance of keeping a daughter *pure* had little, if anything, to do with me. But when I was 14, I definitely had no such understanding.

I knew Vati loved me, but he was always gone. On top of his two jobs, he had started taking evening classes at California State University, Los Angeles. He had decided that to earn more money, he needed more education.

Occasionally, I'd overhear Vati defending me, but Mutti ultimately prevailed. I had to obey my mother, no matter what. "Paradise lies beneath your mother's feet," he'd say, quoting from the Hadith. I tried to remember those words of wisdom, but what I felt from my mother surely wasn't paradise.

I felt left out and left behind. I had four brothers who were in their own worlds. They were free to go out with their friends, free to participate in scouting and sports. I deeply resented the unfairness, day in and day out. I felt so trapped by my identity, or alternatively, by the identity my parents were trying to force upon me.

I felt especially alone because there were no other people around like us, or rather, no one like *me*. I wished I were black, Asian, or Hispanic because then there would be somebody I could relate to, someone I could reach out to.

I wished I were anything but an Arab-Muslim girl. I became more depressed with each passing day and wanted to die. By the time I was 15, I actually thought my life was over. It might have been over had it not been for a major change in our lives.

CHAPTER 5

REBELLION AND ESCAPE

In June 1967, we moved north to Marina, a small community about 10 miles north of Monterey, on California's central coast. Vati's pursuit of further education had paid off. When he finished his course work at Cal State LA, he was offered a position with the Defense Language Institute (DLI) in Monterey where he taught Arabic language and Islamic studies to the US military.

Vati's new job paid well enough that my parents could buy a home. Our family had a new stability that we hadn't known in the US before. But *my* world was more unstable every day. And I was the cause.

My four brothers shared a bedroom—two bunk beds against opposite walls with dressers in between—but I had my own *real* bedroom for the first time since leaving Egypt. I was elated to have my own haven and a door that closed. I thought it was only fair since I'd be spending so much time in there.

Soon after moving in, I became friends with the girls next door, primarily the oldest, Kathy, who was my age. It was nice to have a friend so close, but I was still limited to my own world.

I had been living in a bifurcated household for as long as I could remember: Egyptian and German in addition to the Muslim culture. And now, I had to try and balance the new social norms of the American counterculture of the late 1960s with how my parents expected me to behave. There was already little balance to be had. Civil rights, feminism, radical politics, antiwar protests, marijuana, LSD, and a whole wave of new music—there probably was never a more difficult time than the late sixties to try to reconcile American teenage behavior with conservative Islam.

A Cactus in the Rainforest, a Pine Tree Planted in the Desert

As I got further into my teens, the constraints imposed on me tightened. My parents insisted on strict rules to maintain the Muslim way of life, which still meant no dating without an approved chaperone. As before, those rules applied to me alone. My brothers had no such restrictions—they went out all the time. It was difficult to thrive. I felt like a transplanted cactus or pine tree. I was torn between the Muslim way and the American way in a manner that didn't pertain to my brothers. I considered myself a budding feminist, and it frustrated me to know that I had to work twice as hard as my brothers to be validated as an individual.

Whenever I questioned my parents about the disparity, they told me the same thing: "It's different because you're a girl" or "We worry more about a daughter since her family's reputation depends on her behavior." Trying to convince them that I could make rational decisions for myself same as my brothers could went nowhere. While all the other girls at school were in miniskirts, mine had to be below the knee. I was not allowed to wear makeup or nylon stockings, shave my legs, or even take a purse to school. In my parents' opinion, these common features of American teenage life were off limits, ostensibly because they distracted me from my education. In my teenage mind, I suspected that the underlying reason for these rules was to protect my virginity by making sure I was so unattractive that no boy could possibly be interested in me.

I rebelled. The minute I left the house, I rolled up my skirts at the waist. By the time I got to the bus stop, my skirt was a few inches shorter and I was wearing lipstick. It helped but not enough. I wanted to fit in, but everyone could still tell I was different just by looking at me.

One of my favorite classes in high school was home economics where I learned to sew. I made a beautiful silk necktie for Vati that he wore proudly. Many people complimented me on my natural talent for sewing, which boosted my self-esteem. Although Mutti never took a sewing class and never praised my newfound sewing skills, I often found her trying to teach herself how to sew. I offered to help, hopeful that a shared interest in sewing might become a mother-daughter bonding opportunity—a way to bridge the divide between us—but she consistently turned me down.

US Troubles in a High-School Microcosm

There was a lot of turmoil during my last two years of high school. In essence, Seaside High was a microcosm of the country at large. I didn't fully understand the dynamics of the animosity between the white students and the black students. As an immigrant, I was trying to deal with my own issues and challenges of assimilating.

The Civil Rights Act, which prohibited race-based segregation and discrimination in public facilities, wasn't passed until 1964, when I was 13. But even by the time we'd relocated to Monterey, three years later, it was apparent that changing the law and changing people's hearts was two very different things.

Rick and I were the only Arabs at Seaside High: We didn't "belong" to any of the larger ethnic groups at school. Although I typically didn't like feeling isolated, in the aftermath of the assassination of Dr. Martin Luther King Jr., I was relieved not to be enmeshed in the enmity that I saw all around me.

Vietnam was one issue splitting the country, but the fight for racial equality was a lot more personal in my daily life. There had been repeated skirmishes between white and black students, and one day I found myself in the middle of a mêlée. It had started in the boys' bathroom with a racial slur, spilled out into the hallway, and turned into a free-for-all. I noticed that the white dress I was wearing was heavily stained with blood, and I froze with fear.

This incident shook me to the core as I tried to make sense of what had happened. The blood on my dress wasn't mine. I worried for whoever had been so seriously wounded, and there was no way to tell whether the wounded person was black or white. I realized that this should be a lesson for all of us: Blood is blood, and people are people. Despite the color of our skin, we all bleed the same.

Americans were divided across the country, similar to how we were divided in school. There were demonstrations and protests everywhere. Some had turned violent. Our family did share one fear with the rest of the country: The impending draft. Rick was graduating from high school in June 1968, and we were worried that his number would be called and he'd be sent to war. But Rick was going to college anyway, war or not.

Two months after the assassination of Dr. King, Bobby Kennedy was murdered in the kitchen of the Ambassador Hotel in Los Angeles. He was running for president and had just won the California primary. The assassin, a Palestinian named Sirhan Sirhan, claimed that he killed Kennedy because of Kennedy's strong support for Israel. Everyone in my family was keenly aware of the significance of Bobby Kennedy's assassination. It was the one-year anniversary of the six-day war between the Arabs and the Israelis. We feared that it might generate a backlash against Palestinians and Arabs in the Middle East as well as our family.

* * * * *

My identification with Palestinians and black Americans wasn't only cultural; I felt their pain and anger because the same things had happened to me and my family. We weren't black but we were darker than everyone else in the neighborhoods we lived in and at the schools we attended. We weren't Christian so we had been mocked and bullied because we were "the other."

It was also personal since I felt unfairness and discrimination every day—in my own home. I was denied the freedom my brothers enjoyed. On weekends, while my few friends were spending the night at each other's houses or going to parties or on dates, I wasn't allowed. While my brothers were out having fun with their friends, I was stuck at home, helping Mutti with the cooking and household chores.

It was all done in the name of preserving my innocence. I was often told that "boys only want one thing," which made me furious because the underlying assumption was that I was too dim or helpless to keep them from taking it. To Mutti, remaining a virgin until marriage was paramount. This made me feel that my chastity was the only thing I had going for me and that losing it would render me worthless. "If you ever come home pregnant or I learn that you've lost your virginity before marriage, I will disown you," she said. "And so will your father and your brothers!"

She'd been making this threat since the day I began menstruating. And it worked. Mutti put the fear of God in me, and I dared not stray for fear I would be abandoned by the only family I had, as a result of dishonoring the family reputation.

Sometimes I was able to get out of the house to babysit for a family who lived across the street. Even though it was only 75 cents an hour, I rationalized that the money I earned and saved was the next best thing. In my mind, I was preparing a nest egg for my future freedom.

In the spring of my junior year, I developed a crush on a guy in my class. Jorge was tall with a thick head of straight, black hair and a dimple in his chin. He was very outgoing, yet he could also be serious and quiet at times. I was too shy to tell him just how smitten I was so I considered writing him a letter instead. I talked with Kathy and several other classmates; we giggled about it as girls usually do. I vacillated for weeks about whether to give Jorge the letter or not. Somehow my mother learned of my idea. After school one day, I was in my room when Mutti called out to me from the kitchen. Her tone filled me with fear. *What have I done now?*

"I heard that you've given a love letter to a boy in school?" Mutti asked.

"No, I didn't!" I returned. But fear and its resulting goosebumps popped up over my entire body.

"Yes, you did. I know you did. You can't hide anything from me!" Mutti thundered.

"I did not! How do you know about it anyway?" I answered boldly. I was upset, but I also wanted her to feel that she didn't intimidate me, even though I was deathly afraid of her.

"I have ways of knowing everything you do! Now I know you wrote a letter to a boy and I know you are lying to me!" By this time, she was screaming.

"No, I'm not! I'm not lying to you! I didn't give anyone a love letter!" I cried.

"Yes, you did! I know you did because I have it with me! The letter surfaced to me! You can't lie and hide anything from me!" Mutti continued to bellow. When I heard her say that, I knew she had just lied to me. I knew she didn't have any such letter because I never passed one around to anyone. I had written one and wanted to give it to Jorge, but I hadn't yet; I was too shy and fearful that my parents would find out. I had the letter hidden in one of my drawers, but I hadn't even shown it to anyone. Mutti always warned me that if I ever gave my telephone number to a boy I would be punished "severely."

On top of all the rage, I felt intense anger and disrespect for the fact that she was lying to me. How could my own mother be such a hypocrite?

I rushed back to my bedroom, crying, and slammed the door. I threw myself on my bed and continued to cry in anger and frustration. Before I knew it, my mother opened my bedroom door. As cool as a cucumber yet firm as a two-by-four, she stood in front of my bed with folded arms and ordered me to get up. She was going to teach me "how to properly shut a door."

"No, I'm staying right here!" I cried, through my tears.

"You will get up now or else you will not be allowed to go to Kathy's house or anywhere else!" Mutti said. I stood up. Kathy was really the only friend I had and the only person I was allowed to hang out with. I didn't want to lose that one speck of privilege. Mutti then walked from my bed to the door and quietly closed it as if demonstrating step-by-step instructions to a toddler. Her condescension angered me even more.

"Now you can give me a return demonstration of how to close a door properly," she said. I grabbed the doorknob and slammed the door as hard as I could. My mother was startled but ultimately unaffected. She repeated her demonstration and asked me to try again. I slammed the door shut once more. This went on for two more rounds before Mutti gave me a beating and grounded me for two weeks. This didn't bother me as much as the fact that my mother had lied to me and I wasn't brave enough to tell her I knew. Instead I was embarrassed for her and wrestled with how I was going to tell her because I didn't want her to feel humiliated and become angrier.

I never said a word to her about this incident until many years later. My mother said she didn't have any recollection of this confrontation. My relationship with my mother remained strained for the rest of my life.

I often reflected on and compared my relationship with my grandmother to that with my mother. Back in Cairo, spending time with grandmother was one way I compensated for the lack of affection I felt from Mutti. For example, when I baked with grandmother, she carefully explained all the steps in each recipe with such love and patience.

Her soft voice and loving touch comforted me. One evening while we were sitting together on the balcony of her villa, clouds diffused the light from the setting sun, creating soft orange and pink hues in the sky.

"You see those beautiful, soft, orange clouds out there?" my grandmother asked, pointing to the sky.

"Yes," I replied, watching in awe.

"Whenever the sky appears this way, it means the angels are baking in heaven," she told me. I have held on to that belief throughout my life and have passed it on to my own children—it's one way for me to keep the memories of my beloved grandmother alive.

She listened with complete attention as I told her stories, and she happily answered all my questions. Better yet, she knew the answers I needed to hear. With my grandmother, nothing I said was trivial. Whatever I talked about mattered to her.

My grandmother sensed my sadness whenever I'd been spanked or scolded by Mutti. She consistently expressed her unconditional love for me, and knowing how much she cared about me was a great boost to my bruised self-esteem.

My perpetual dream was to have a bond such as this with my mother, but we just couldn't get along. For as long as I can remember, my relationship with Mutti was a constant battle of personalities and wills, and she always won because I was the child…the girl child.

My father was firm with regards to cultural values as well, but he went about it in a softer, milder, manner. Rather than imposing rule and law, Vati explained the rationale for retaining our cultural values. But it was absolutely impossible for me to understand this because there weren't any other girls in my situation. I had no one to identify with or hang out with aside from Kathy. I was convinced back then that even my friendship with Kathy was only allowed because she lived next door; my parents knew her parents and they could still monitor me.

Culturally speaking, I felt unappreciated and isolated. Once again, I wished I belonged to another ethnic group. I wanted to be black, Hispanic, or Asian. They all had their tight-knit communities and support systems. I wished I were anything but Egyptian, Arab, or Muslim. I never thought my brothers felt this way because they seemed to partake in lots of activities with friends with minimal restrictions.

"But how will I ever meet anyone who I'll want to marry someday if I'm not allowed to date?" I kept asking, only to receive the perennial reply that dating was forbidden without the presence of a chaperone and that I was to marry a Muslim when the time came. Period! No discussion here. It was frustrating and confusing to me because I had no other societal examples or role models in my life.

Our New Islamic Family Routine

Within a few months after our arrival to Monterey, Vati and some of his colleagues at the DLI started an Islamic center since there weren't any around, to our knowledge. We met at homes every Friday evening and each family took a turn hosting.

The last time I had been to a mosque was when I was a child living in Saudi Arabia. Other than me and Mutti, there were only a few other women in attendance. We left our shoes by the door, and the women wrapped their heads with scarves to cover their hair and wore clothing that covered the entire body except for their face, hands, and feet.

Men and women prayed in separate areas but here the women prayed behind the men. This bothered me and made me feel inferior to my brothers once again. I didn't want to pray *behind* them; I wanted to pray *next* to them. I had no choice, however, but to comply. For me, this was another cactus in the rainforest, pine tree in the desert moment, putting my Muslim self in direct conflict with the empowered American female self I was striving to become.

I complained and Vati sat me down to explain it. "The reason why women are obliged to remain behind the men is to keep the men from being distracted by looking at the women in front of them, thus preventing them from concentrating on prayer."

"Well, the men should control their thoughts," I said.

"It's not that simple, *ya habibti,* my darling," Vati replied with a playful grin. "Since prayers involve bowing from the waist and kneeling down, the men could easily become distracted by watching the women's behinds."

I didn't buy the explanation. To me, it raised more questions than it answered. Why were men so hopelessly unable to control themselves? And above all, why should women be held responsible for men's impure thoughts?

Now We're the Arabs Once Again

In our neighborhood, it was well known that we were Arabs—thanks to my parents' heavy accents. There was one family that took a particular dislike to us. It's still hard to understand why they hated us so much since I'd heard the mom speak German to Mutti when we first moved in. They had two sons and a daughter who were all a little older than me.

They lived on the other side of Kathy's house. One hot summer afternoon, Kathy and I were in her front yard, running through the sprinklers, and intermittently hosing each other down in an effort to beat the heat. We were giggling, having fun, and minding our own business when one of the sons pulled into his driveway next door. He stood there briefly, staring at us. A few moments later, he mumbled something. Kathy and I couldn't make out what he'd said and asked him to speak louder. "You dirty little Arab slut," he shouted at the top of his voice. "Go back to your filthy tent where you belong!"

Arab slut...me? I thought. I must have been the only girl in Seaside High who had never been kissed or even held hands with a boy. All my anger with discrimination boiled over. I grabbed the hose and acted on my first impulse—to defend my honor and my reputation.

I opened the spigot and cranked up the water pressure. Then I aimed the hose nozzle straight at his crotch. Bullseye! He yelped in pain then ran toward us. I dropped the hose, and Kathy and I sprinted for her house, slamming the front door just in time. Or so we thought.

He crashed right through it and came at me, shouted the slurs again. Then he slugged me in the head. After I fell to the floor, he kicked me repeatedly, then ran off as soon as he realized Kathy's dad was in the next room. Someone called the police.

I was still in Kathy's living room when the police arrived. My family showed up as well. They were shocked when they saw the gigantic welt on my forehead and heard what happened. My brothers and their friends wanted to hunt the boy down and take revenge. Not Vati. When the officers asked him if he wanted to press charges, Vati hastily replied, "No." He said he was going to file a report but that was all. I was furious. Why would he not seek justice on my behalf? Kathy's dad spoke up and said he intended to press charges against the boy for trespassing.

I felt betrayed by my own father. Wasn't what happened to me a crime? "I don't want any more trouble," Vati explained when we got home. "Maybe filing a report will be enough of a warning that he doesn't do this again."

I rushed into my room, slammed the door, and cried, questioning my value and self-worth. With my forehead injury and the bruises on my back, I looked as bad as I felt. My injuries would take weeks to heal. It was like what happened in St. Louis but somehow this time my father thought that it didn't matter—that *I* didn't matter. I came to the conclusion that I was less important than the door to Kathy's house that the kid had busted through.

I never knew what happened to the trespassing complaint that Kathy's father had initiated, but years later, Vati explained why he didn't press charges. At the time, he was applying for a government security clearance. It would expand his career opportunities, and he didn't want the incident to affect his chances. I was relieved to learn that the background check was the real reason why Vati said he didn't want to make trouble, but I would have felt much better if he'd told me back then.

The year 1969 ushered in a new epoch, filled with news stories that would forever change the fabric of America. The ongoing and painful Vietnam war, the Stonewall riots in New York City, the moon landing, the grisly Manson murders, the death of Ho Chi Minh (with the hopes of an end to the war), and Woodstock. But the biggest story for me was my high school graduation. I would finally be allowed to get my driver's license and take on summer work to earn a regular income—one of my first steps to freedom. I landed a full-time job at Macy's and was now permitted to leave the house for my job and education.

I worked primarily in Macy's fabric department, and I loved it. My employment also represented an opportunity to combat the extremely conservative dress restrictions my parents still tried to impose upon me. I fought back harder than ever, insisting that I should be able to wear whatever I wanted. Eventually, my parents started to give way a little—perhaps they grew weary of my complaining and protesting or perhaps they began to realize that they couldn't keep me bottled up at home forever.

I made myself a brand new, stylish wardrobe using the sewing skills I had learned in high school and the latest fabrics I found in Macy's. I even made Pendleton plaid wool shirts for each of my brothers as Christmas gifts. They all said they loved their shirts, and hearing that gave me a tremendous feeling of being loved and appreciated. I hung on to these bits of positive validation whenever they came my way.

MONTEREY PENINSULA COLLEGE: A DIVERSE EXPERIENCE

My parents were adamant that I go to college. "I brought you to *Amreeka* so you would have the opportunity for higher education," Vati said. "You can consider any career you want, but you must have your degree in hand first." Years later, I understood the wisdom of his words.

Like many little girls, I loved ballet and had dreamed of being a dancer ever since I took classes in Cairo. But there was no such opportunity in Saudi Arabia. And in America, my parents simply couldn't afford lessons or classes. I also wanted to become a pilot like my Onkel Rolf but as a woman that was unattainable as well. Then I became interested in nursing after learning about the profession through friends.

A classmate talked about becoming an Air Force nurse after she graduated from college. That sounded like something I might want to do. I thought that I could perhaps join the Air Force as a nurse and eventually realize my dream to become a pilot. My parents approved, to my surprise. With their full support, I began taking science prerequisites that would lead to a degree in nursing.

Both Rick and I went to Monterey Peninsula College (MPC). We met foreign students from all over the world, including students from the Middle East and Asia. My brother and I joined the newly formed Arab-American club on campus, which gave us the opportunity to socialize with our fellow Arab students and become reacquainted with Arab culture. It felt good to reconnect with a part of our heritage, especially after so many years of rejection by mainstream Americans. We even learned to dance the *dabke*, a Lebanese folk dance, and we performed as a club group for various celebrations. As usual, I was only allowed to participate in these dances because Rick was there.

One of my favorite classes at MPC was US black history. My high school American history textbooks had ignored the topic of slavery altogether. In this class, I learned about the ongoing struggle for civil rights and Dr. Martin Luther King Jr.'s "I Have a Dream" speech. I was the *lightest* skinned person in my class, which meant I was considered the only *white* person taking the course.

How would I be defined? The absurdity of "judging others by the color of their skin and not the content of their character" hit me harder the more I learned in that particular class.

Sister Gabriel and My Ticket to Freedom

A petite young woman in my chemistry class introduced herself as "Sister Gabriel." She was a nun, and she came to class in a long black robe with a starched white collar around her neck. A black veil with white trim covered her head and framed her cute, round face. A fringe of dark brown bangs peeked out from underneath. I'd never met a nun before, but Sister Gabriel was most approachable. I wanted to know more about her clothing, which seemed quite similar to the *abaya* worn in countries like Saudi Arabia.

"It's called a habit," Sister Gabriel told me, smiling.

"Why do you have to wear it?" I asked.

"Because I'm a nun. It's our 'uniform' and a way to display our modesty," she replied. She went on to explain that although she was a Franciscan nun, she was also a licensed vocational nurse (LVN) and worked in a convalescent hospital for sick and elderly nuns. She wanted to become a registered nurse (RN), which was why she was taking courses at MPC.

Both of us struggled with chemistry so we began studying together. These study sessions were the beginning of a close friendship. Sister Gabriel was as curious about my background as I was about hers. Over the course of the semester, we began to hang out more frequently.

We initially studied at my house, but I was soon allowed to visit her at the convent. Eventually, Sister Gabriel snuck me into her room, which was located in the cloisters, the innermost private area of the convent. Her room was tiny, barely big enough for a single bed, a nightstand, and a dresser but it was cozy. There was a crucifix on the wall above her bed and a small rug on the floor. The only other possessions I could see were a few books on her dresser, standing neatly between two bookends. A small, framed picture of Jesus and Mary stood next to the books and that was it.

Sister Gabriel explained that as a nun, one of the vows she took was that of poverty, which is why she didn't need anything else. "All my essentials are provided for. Living here in the convent, I'm not in need of anything," she said.

"Don't you get lonely sometimes?" I asked her.

"No, I'm married to Jesus," Sister Gabriel replied as she showed me her plain silver wedding band.

I'd never heard of that before. She told me she'd been a nun for nine years but had yet to take her final vows.

Sister Gabriel began visiting our house regularly. She met my parents and brothers, and before long she expressed her fondness for my entire family. My parents accepted her with open hearts and open minds.

I'm sure being named Sister Gabriel didn't hurt in terms of winning my parents over. "She's named Sister Gabriel, after the angel Gabriel," Vati said, reminding me that the angel Gabriel (*Jabril* in Arabic) appeared before *Mother Miriam* (PBUH) and proclaimed to her that she would give birth to Prophet *Issa*, Jesus (PBUH). Angel Gabriel also appeared before Prophet Muhammed (PBUH) to inspire the revelation of the Qur'an. And it was *Jabril* who led Prophet Muhammed from Mecca to the Al Aqsa mosque in Jerusalem during *Leilat el mirage*—the night journey. As far as my parents were concerned, Sister Gabriel was worthy of becoming a part of the family. The fact that we were Muslims and she was a Catholic nun was never an issue.

So when Sister Gabriel decided against being a nun, and needed a place to live, I invited her to stay with us while she made her way back into the everyday secular world. Naturally, I got my parents' permission first.

Sister Gabriel reclaimed her birth name, Janie. She stayed with us for the rest of the school year. I shared my room with her, and we became close friends—she was the sister I never had. And like sisters, we shared secrets and exchanged clothes. And we went shopping—after nine years in the convent, she didn't have anything to wear.

I was surprised to see how well Janie got along with Mutti. She was skilled at putting out fires when my mother and I couldn't see eye to eye. She also helped me with many of my chores, which meant I had more free time and freedom to go out.

I could go anywhere, as long as I went with Janie. It didn't take long for me to realize that the only reason this was allowed was because my parents felt Janie was "safe and pure"—the perfect companion for me. After all, she'd been a nun! With Janie's help, I was finally feeling a little liberated from the oppression at home.

But what my parents didn't know was that Janie was also enjoying her newfound freedom, and she was as bold and adventurous as me.

On beautiful warm days, we skipped classes and drove to Pebble Beach or Big Sur, enjoying our freedom on the beaches and in the sunshine. At other times, we went to the theater and watched movies all day long. These adventures were our little secret.

The following year, I was accepted as a transfer student at San Francisco State University where I could complete my nursing education. I chose SFSU because their program would enable me to get my bachelor's degree. Perhaps more importantly, it was beyond commuting distance from home so I had to live on campus. It was my ticket out of the house and my escape from my mother's relentless control. Janie moved to San Jose where she was able to live close to her family and continue her studies.

CHAPTER 6

TORN BETWEEN
MANY ISLAMS

"Free at last! Thank God almighty, free at last!" Getting my own dorm room wasn't at all what Dr. Martin Luther King Jr. had in mind when he gave his "I Have a Dream" speech, but I knew exactly what he meant.

I felt liberated and exhilarated. I was finally on my own, no longer under my parents' rules and restrictions. On the Saturday before registration and orientation, my parents drove me to San Francisco. They were as sad as I was elated. After helping me get settled in my dorm room, my teary-eyed father reminded me of our "cultural behavioral rules" as "Won't Get Fooled Again" by The Who blared through one of the open dorm windows.

As soon as they left, I literally jumped up and down for joy.

San Francisco was Ground Zero for the music I loved, feminism, and opposition to the Vietnam War. Student demonstrations at SFSU were frequent—there were marches, rallies, and sit-ins, and police were often summoned to the campus to break them up.

I was reluctant to participate, even though I shared the protestors' sentiments. I wanted to stay focused on my studies, and I was also afraid of what would happen if my parents found out. I did fully embrace the counterculture, however. I was one of the flower children, and I dressed in long flowing skirts, peasant blouses, and sandals. My hair was thick and long, halfway down my back and parted down the middle, often ringed with a fresh flower garland around my head.

SFSU was challenging and I found the course work demanding. Whenever I became discouraged, I would call Vati for inspiring pep talks. "In this country, you can achieve your highest dreams..." His coaching was usually all I needed to get back on track.

I developed many new friendships and felt as though I was beginning to be on equal footing with my peers. My social circle included young men and women of all religions and ethnic backgrounds, and it felt good to be accepted into a group of friends where race, religion, or national origin didn't matter. The weekend was party time and that included both alcohol and marijuana. My friends and I became a roving party, going from one dorm room to another, grooving away into the early hours of the morning.

I began dating at SFSU but most of the relationships ended quickly since I never felt comfortable going all the way. This was the early 1970s, and by now sex was sort of expected, especially in San Francisco—everything in the counterculture promoted free love and casual sexual relations.

It seemed like I was the only one not sleeping with someone, but my Muslim background and ultra-sheltered upbringing prevented me from indulging. I kissed and made out but I never went any further. As a result, some guys branded me as "the girl who doesn't put out" and "a prick teaser." I couldn't shake the idea that Mutti had drummed into my brain —that losing my virginity before marriage was a transgression so serious it would bring shame on the entire family and result in me being ostracized forever. Vati never threatened me like Mutti did, but he did regularly remind me that we were Muslims and "we don't do that."

An exception was a guy I'd consider marrying. I told Mutti about him when I was home collecting some of my belongings to bring back to school. In disbelief, my mother sternly asked me if he was a Muslim.

"Of course not. There aren't any Muslims here except us," I replied.

"He'll need to convert to Islam before you marry him," she said.

"He probably doesn't even know what Islam is," I said.

"Well then, that settles it. You have to marry a Muslim because no other man will ever respect you!" my mother insisted.

"What's so special about being a Muslim anyway? All of our friends are Christians, and they're good people! What makes us so special that we can't marry anyone outside of Islam?" I retorted furiously.

Annoyed and angry, I packed up my things and drove away. I felt like I didn't even want to come home anymore. I was still being treated like a child who was incapable of making her own decisions. I just couldn't understand the concept that no man would respect me unless he was Muslim.

During the summer of 1973, I stayed in San Francisco to work full time in order to pay for my upcoming year's college expenses. Mostly though, I didn't want to come home.

One afternoon while riding my bike in San Francisco's Mission District, I came upon a store that had a sign advertising halal meats and chicken. *Halal* in Arabic literally means "permissible." *Haram*, the opposite term, means "forbidden." Taken from the Qur'an, these two common Islamic terms are most often used to describe foods and beverages, but they can also refer to clothing, cosmetics, medications, finances, recreation, and life in general.

Wow! I thought to myself. *Halal?* I entered the store and saw several black men wearing skullcaps and long white gowns, not unlike what Saudi men wore. We exchanged greetings as I passed them and went straight to the meat counter to inquire about the halal meats and how they knew what halal was. One of the men told me he was Muslim. Feeling an instant connection, I announced that I was Muslim, too, and told them that I didn't think there could be enough Muslims living in San Francisco to devote an entire store to halal meats. Puzzled, they glanced at each other. After a few seconds, one of them came up to me and said, "Can't be! You're *white!*" He explained that they were members of the Nation of Islam, a religious black separatist organization that followed the religious teachings of Elijah Muhammed. That statement made my identity even more confusing.

I was mystified and said that according to the Qur'an, Islam is colorblind. The teachings of Prophet Muhammed (*not* Elijah Muhammed) didn't distinguish who could or could not become a Muslim based on skin color. "We as human beings created by God are meant to be different and diverse. Different colors, races, languages. Whether black, white, yellow, brown, or whatever, we are all part of the natural order of God's creations," I declared. "And I'm not white!" It bothered me that my identity jumped from one polar opposite to another depending on the day and who I met. Instead of debating with them further, I purchased some items and bid them farewell.

A few months later, while enjoying my new freedom, I was dealt an appalling reality check once more. One of Vati's friends, a Muslim from Burma, conducted my brother Rick's traditional Islamic wedding. I was denied the opportunity to be one of the two witnesses needed to sign the wedding documents, unless another woman signed along with me. I later asked Vati to explain the rationale for this requirement. Vati quoted from the Qur'an: "And ye get two witnesses out of your own men. And if there are not two men, then a man and two women, such as ye choose for witnesses, so that if one of them errs, the other can remind her." When I challenged him about it, he tried to explain the underlying reasoning, which was that a woman's emotions can often affect her decisions.

A woman's signature is worth one-half of a man's? Really? The fact that my inferiority as a woman had been enshrined in the most sacred teachings of my religion only added to my feelings of inequality. I considered myself a feminist, and I wouldn't and couldn't bring myself to accept this archaic rule.

At SFSU, I'd become active in the feminist movement. I rallied for equal rights and equal pay. But now, I finally understood that it would be an ongoing struggle for me to be recognized as anything more than half a person.

VATI'S LIFELONG FRIEND, ANWAR SADAT

My parents returned to Egypt to visit for the first time since we fled 15 years earlier. It was finally safe to go back—Gamal Abdel Nasser was dead, and the new president was Vati's lifelong friend, Anwar Sadat. Over the years, the two had maintained their friendship through clandestine letters. Now my parents returned to a warm reunion with the president and his wife, Jehan. In Vati's words, "It was like coming home again." President Sadat honored my father by reinstating him to the same elite position in the police department that he'd held before he left with an honorary promotion to the highest rank possible. President Sadat also included all retroactive salary from the time Vati abruptly had had to flee, until the day he and Vati were reunited. Going forward, my father was also to receive his full monthly pension for the remainder of his life. But the money had to stay in Egypt, so Vati used it to support his mother (our Teta) and other relatives still living in Cairo.

On October 6, 1973, Egypt and Syria joined forces in a surprise attack on Israel in an effort to regain the territory seized by the Israelis in 1967. Iraq and Jordan soon joined in. What became known as the Yom Kippur War lasted for 19 days and vied for the headlines with Senate hearings on the Watergate break-in and cover-up. The Arabs had great military success initially but after the US resupplied Israel, they eventually turned the tide. In retaliation, Saudi Arabia and other Arab members of the Organization of the Petroleum Exporting Countries (OPEC), plus Egypt and Syria, officially declared an oil embargo against the US, Canada, the United Kingdom, the Netherlands, and Japan—the countries that had assisted Israel. Gas prices in the States soared—if you could find gas, that is. Long lines formed at the pumps.

My family and I were keenly aware of all of these events—and not from the news alone. When the embargo began, Vati was in Riyadh on assignment from the US Department of Defense (DOD). My father had also maintained his relationship with Ahmed Zaki Yamani, the man who helped us while we lived in exile in Saudi Arabia. Yamani had since been granted the title of Sheik and had become Saudi Arabia's minister of oil and minerals. Sheik Yamani, my father's dear friend, was now leading the oil embargo.

During the time we lived in Monterey, Vati earned his master's and PhD in Arabic and Middle Eastern Studies. Shortly after that, the DOD tapped him to be the US liaison to assist with the modernization of the Saudi Arabian National Guard (SANG). He worked closely with Saudi Arabia's minister of defense, Prince Abdullah (later King Abdullah). This was the job of my father's dreams, one that would take him back to a culture in which he felt comfortable, this time as a US citizen. And it was the same job my father was offered after applying for the government security clearance when I was in high school.

Mutti and my youngest brother, Ralph, joined him as soon as he got settled in the newly built, gated American community. During their tour in Saudi Arabia, Ralph and my parents made their *Hajj*, the pilgrimage to Mecca, which is one of the five pillars of Islam.

Shortly after Mutti left for Saudi Arabia, I received a telephone call from a young man who spoke English with a heavy Egyptian/Arabic accent. I knew immediately who he was because Mutti had informed me that she passed on my telephone number to a family friend to give to the young man now on the telephone. She didn't tell Vati of her attempts at matchmaking.

The young man was polite and seemed hesitant as he explained how he had acquired my telephone number. He said his name was Nadir Mohamed. He was a 25-year-old foreign student at Berkeley. He was from Cairo, Egypt, and he was a Muslim.

After several evenings talking on the phone, we went to lunch at a local San Francisco restaurant. He was average, about 5 feet, 11 inches tall with dark brown, penetrating eyes and very short, dark brown, kinky hair. His outfit made him peculiar: a white shirt with long sleeves rolled halfway up his arm, brown baggy trousers, and brown leather dress shoes.

My first hunch was that I didn't care for him. Then he lit a cigarette, which was an immediate turnoff. And it became clear that his main focus—his *only* focus—was on getting his master's degree in engineering. Berkeley was and is part of the University of California system, and I knew that as a foreign student, he was paying a lot more in tuition than California residents. When the subject came up, he assured me that this was not a problem for him since he was covered by student loans and received a regular monthly stipend as a research assistant. He told me that he had more than enough money, not only to pay tuition but also live comfortably.

Nadir didn't ask me about any of my interests, my studies in nursing, or my plans for the future. It was a very boring, one-sided conversation. He struck me as strange and a bit full of himself, and I asked him to take me home after we finished our meal.

I figured that was the end of it, until he called to ask me out to dinner. Since I wasn't interested in him, I declined, saying that I already had a boyfriend. I lied.

Several weeks went by before I heard from Nadir again. Then one evening, I received a telephone call. "Hello, Miss Mona?" the voice asked meekly.

"Yes," I replied.

"This is Nadir." His quiet, reserved tone and stuttering suggested that he was very nervous.

"Nadir who?" I asked. I didn't want to sound excited or happy to hear from him again. The truth was that I was sorry I picked up the phone. I was quite surprised that he'd called me again. Now, however, I felt a little guilty about blowing him off and lying to him about having a boyfriend. I decided to give him another chance.

We started dating. He took me to dinner, to the movies, and for walks in Golden Gate Park; he always behaved like a perfect gentleman. He still smoked but he put his cigarette out as soon as I let him know that the smoke burned my eyes. I thought he was very nice, polite, and seemingly educated, but I didn't feel anything like what most people describe as butterflies.

But then again, what did I know of butterflies? I had never felt them because I'd never been in love before. In terms of dating experience, I was at least six or seven years behind other young women my age.

During Christmas break in 1973, Nadir proposed to me. He said he'd like to marry me as soon as possible because he was very much in love with me and just knew I was the one for him. He was full of promises. He promised to always treat me like a jewel. He promised to always protect me. He even promised to stop smoking. Most important to me, Nadir promised to allow me to follow my dream—my career—wherever that might take me.

Over the next few months, I began thinking about whether Nadir would be a suitable husband. I compared him to Vati, the finest man I knew. Like my father, he was Egyptian and Muslim, both definite pluses. I was very close to my father and always felt that he was a good, honest, kind, and loving man who treated my mother with utmost respect and loyalty. Nadir had treated me with great respect so far—could it be that Nadir was like Vati and that he would treat me like my father treated my mother?

I also started thinking a lot about the problem of scarcity. The number of eligible young Muslim men in the Bay Area was tiny. Since starting college, I had met very few Muslim guys and exactly zero Egyptians. How many others were going to come my way? My parents had always emphasized the importance of marrying a Muslim man and this was my opportunity. My mother had arranged for me to meet Nadir—could it be that her choice was the right one for me? I desperately wanted to please my parents. Despite the absence of butterflies, I wanted to do what was right out of a sense of obligation to my faith and to my family—what I had been trained and conditioned to accept as the proper thing to do.

Despite pressure from Nadir to get married right away, I told him that I wasn't going to marry anyone until I'd graduated from college. In May 1974, with graduation fast approaching, we got engaged. I had planned the engagement for May because I knew my parents would be arriving home on leave from Saudi Arabia for my brother John's wedding in June. Ever since my parents left for Riyadh, John had been living in the house in Marina with his then-girlfriend. For me, even the idea of that arrangement was a sore subject. John was openly doing what I had been absolutely forbidden to do, but by this time I knew that the family double standard was nothing more than a way to keep me in line and under control.

We had a small, informal engagement party at the house in Marina. Although I had spoken about Nadir with my parents when they called from Saudi Arabia, this was their first meeting. After talking to Nadir at length about his family, goals, and future plans, Vati seemed extremely uneasy. He didn't tell me what his specific concerns were, only that he didn't have good feelings about the man I was going to marry. Mutti just sat there, quiet and unruffled. Nadir and I spent the night in Marina: I stayed in my bedroom and he slept on the couch in the living room.

The next day, I went for a short walk with Vati. It was a beautiful late morning, sunny and warm, and our neighborhood was teeming with children playing and riding their bikes everywhere. We had a good long chat about Nadir.

"How long have you known Nadir?" my father asked.

"Since last fall, right after Mutti left for Saudi Arabia," I answered.

"Why do you want to marry him?" Vati gingerly asked.

His question caught me off guard, and I paused before answering. "He is a very nice young man and very smart. He's Egyptian and a Muslim, and I know you and Mutti want me to marry a Muslim, right?" I struggled to find the right words—but I was unable to lie to my father and say that I was in love with him.

"And how did you meet him?" Vati finally asked.

I looked at him with surprise—surely, he already knew the answer to his own question.

"Mutti gave Mr. Simopoulos my telephone number to give to him," I replied.

"What?" Vati's distress was obvious—he was stunned to learn that Mutti had done this without his knowledge and that it had led to my engagement.

I was totally confused at this point. I had grown up knowing I was supposed to marry a Muslim man. Now here was a young, educated Egyptian Muslim man who wanted to marry me and yet my father was troubled.

Vati remained quiet and pensive as we walked home. Later that afternoon, in a private conversation with me and Mutti, he indicated that he was furious at my mother for going behind his back to do this. Mutti defended herself, insisting—as she had throughout my adolescence—that she didn't care who I married as long as he was a Muslim.

Once again, rules that applied to me didn't apply to my brothers. They were free to marry outside the faith, since it was assumed that their wives would convert to Islam and therefore all of their children would be Muslims. Needless to say, it didn't work out that way at all.

I thought again about my rationale. On the one hand, there were so few educated, available young Muslim men that I worried I might never meet another one. On the other hand, I could see how upset Vati was. He obviously had some serious reservations about Nadir but he didn't give me any specifics. In the end, my father gave Nadir the benefit of the doubt and went along with approving the engagement.

A few weeks after graduating from SFSU and after taking the California state nursing board exam, I moved into Nadir's Berkeley apartment. He had persuaded me that it would be the most logical thing to do. For young people who weren't raised as conservatively as I was, this was absolutely normal. People in their twenties were living together not only before marriage but also without any intention of ever getting married at all.

Many of my college friends were living together. I wanted to do the same, to essentially "test-drive" the relationship before making a final commitment. But when my parents learned that I had moved in with Nadir, they were livid. They insisted that I move out immediately. Even though we were engaged with their blessing, they found it highly improper for me to be living in a man's apartment until I was married.

Nadir wasted no time turning this problem into an opportunity. Agreeing with my parents, he suggested that we get married right away so that we weren't "living in sin." I was gullible and naïve, and Nadir was persuasive and insistent.

Nadir's place was a small, one-bedroom apartment in Berkeley that was within walking distance of the campus. Berkeley had a lot in common with SFSU in that there always seemed to be a circus of political and social activity. At Sather Gate off Telegraph Avenue, you could see everything from anti-Vietnam War protestors to a shirtless guy in leather pants who thinks he's Jim Morrison of the Doors to Hare Krishna devotees with their drums, temple bells, and tambourines.

In August 1974, Nadir and I went to the Alameda County Courthouse to get married. I was 22 and he was 26. Rick, John, and their wives attended the ceremony, and they all stood in as our witnesses. I was suddenly a married woman with a Muslim husband. This was my chance to finally be equal to my brothers. Or so I thought.

For the next seven years, life was hell.

PART II

CHAPTER 7

THE REAL NADIR

We all returned to our Berkeley apartment after the ceremony.

For dinner, I had prepared for a traditional Egyptian feast—*warak enab* (stuffed grape leaves), cucumber and yogurt salad, *tabouli, kibbi, koufta, shish kebab*, Egyptian rice, *konafa, baklawa,* and *molokhiya*. I had mastered all of these dishes, with the exception of molokhiya, because I had often cooked them at home when I was growing up. Mutti always chose to make molokhiya herself and she made it frequently. I had never attempted to cook it before, but since Nadir told me molokhiya was one of his favorite dishes, I went ahead and made it for the first time.

Molokhiya is a thick, dark green soup with a smooth, slimy texture similar to overcooked okra. Its name is derived from the Arabic word for king, and in ancient times it was reserved for pharaohs and nobles. Today it's considered one of the national dishes of Egypt. Jute leaves are the key ingredient and they're cooked in a broth, usually chicken. It's tricky to prepare because first it must be brought almost to a boil and then left to simmer.

The key word is "almost"—if molokhiya boils, it separates and becomes watery. As I was setting the table and taking care of last-minute details for dinner, I got distracted and forgot the molokhiya on the stove. It boiled and separated.

I was upset that I'd ruined the dish, but Rick tried to console me. "Oh well," he said. "I'm sure it will taste fine. Let's eat it anyway."

Everyone else was also supportive—this was, after all, a wedding celebration. Everyone, that is, except Nadir. While Rick, John, and their wives enjoyed their soup, Nadir remained quiet. Finally, wearing a poker face, he spoke in Arabic. "*Eh el khara da?*" he said. "What is this shit?" Nadir chuckled, then he dumped the molokhiya onto the plate set beneath his bowl, soiling the linen tablecloth I had so meticulously ironed the previous day.

No one else was amused. My brothers and I exchanged worried glances. I was especially mortified because I knew that my brothers understood Arabic too. Fighting back tears, I picked up Nadir's bowl, cleaned up the mess, and set a fresh place for him.

* * * * *

In late fall 1974, I took the California State Board of Nursing exam at the Oakland Coliseum. While I waited for the results, which normally took about three months, I landed a part-time job at a plasma center in Berkeley as a graduate nurse. Right around the new year 1975, I received an envelope with my registered nurse license inside. Great news! I jumped up and down.

"I passed! I passed!" I shouted excitedly to Nadir, who was sitting in a recliner reading a textbook.

"That's nice," Nadir responded without looking up at me. Based on that reaction, it was difficult to discern how he truly felt about it.

I applied for jobs all over the Berkeley-Oakland area, and in March 1975, I accepted a staff nurse position at Merritt Hospital in Oakland. New RNs are on the lowest rung of the nursing hierarchy—and I was assigned the night shift. I worked with another RN named Norma, who became a close, lifelong friend. I was happy to have a job that got me out of the apartment because my home life was once again more sad than happy.

Nadir was not the same person I dated only a few months earlier. He criticized everything I did—my cooking, my cleaning, my ironing, and even my driving. He became more possessive and controlling, all the while telling me how much he loved me. He blamed his behavior on the stress and pressure of his graduate studies. I thought things would get better.

A few months later, we were in the car. Nadir was driving and noticed that I smiled at a man in the car next to us while we were stopped at a red light. Nadir's face flushed and the vein in his temple pulsed.

"What are you looking at?" he asked.

"I was just smiling to say hello to the guy in the next car," I replied.

"Don't you know that as a married woman, it's *haram* for you to look at or smile at other men?"

"Oh, that's ridiculous," I said with a laugh. I honestly thought he was kidding—until Nadir jammed his elbow—hard—into my left arm. I yelped in pain. He ignored me. I let it go for the moment but when we returned home, I complained. There was already a large bruise on my aching arm. After a few hours, Nadir apologized.

Criticism. Abuse. Apology. The pattern was established, and it would play out, day after day. This back and forth between abuse and remorse was extremely difficult for me to process.

* * * * *

Several months later, in January 1975, my parents came home for our formal wedding ceremony. It was a simple, yet traditional

Islamic wedding where my father proudly walked me down the aisle in their home in Marina.

"Bism Allah Alrahman Alrahim," my father said while holding his Qur'an. "In the name of God, most gracious, most merciful." Vati then recited verses pertaining to marriage. Our family, closest friends, and neighbors witnessed the short ritual, which resembles Western Christian weddings. Standing next to me, aloof and almost detached when speaking to Vati, Nadir was putting up a façade for everyone. I knew it and my brothers didn't buy his sudden tranquil demeanor either.

Although they were invited, no one from Nadir's side was there—not his Berkeley friends, not his older brother, Sammon (who at the time was working and living in Delaware with his wife, Brenda), not his parents. I thought that was rather odd. My family thought so too.

Because of Nadir's impassive affect and explosive temper, I already had deep-seated feelings of regret. I was sorry that we were already legally married. In my heart, I wanted to cancel the traditional ceremony and rethink my future, but I didn't have the courage to tell my family how unhappy I was. I didn't want to embarrass them or myself with my change of heart.

* * * * *

Nadir applied for permanent resident status as soon as we were married. Despite his prenuptial reassurances that he was self-sufficient, I ended up paying for most of our expenses, including his tuition.

Nadir was a chain smoker, and he insisted on smoking in the apartment, reneging on his promises to quit. My eyes burned constantly. He also drank two or three bottles of beer each evening—and it had to be imported, not American. Even though I was working full time, we were still struggling financially, so I brought up the subject of his cigarettes and imported beer as extra expenses we couldn't afford. Each time I mentioned this topic, it turned into a heated argument. True to the pattern, I would cry and he would apologize. And then things would get better.

Nadir liked to spend money—more money than he could make because I was the breadwinner. When I went to balance the checkbook each month, I found bunches of canceled checks, all written for cash in amounts ranging from 10 to 50 dollars. He'd promise, "When I receive my graduate degree and have a good job, I will pay you back—every cent and even more!" Once again, I believed him.

And then I began fielding phone calls from women asking to speak to Nadir. When I asked him who they were, he said they were fellow graduate students and research assistants. I believed him—until there was a knock on our apartment door late one night. A scantily dressed blonde stood in the doorway.

"Hi. Is Nadir home?" she asked. Nadir was indeed home, but he didn't come to the door, choosing instead to hide in the bathroom.

"Who are you?" I asked in disbelief.

"I'm Sharon. Who are you?" the woman replied.

"I'm Nadir's wife," I boldly stated.

"What? So the guy got hooked up? Wow!"

"How do you know my husband?"

I could tell she was drunk; her speech was slurred as she explained that Nadir paid her for sexual services. As she continued talking, I felt my heart beat faster and my blood pressure rise. When she started to walk away, I slammed the door and turned to Nadir, who by then figured it was safe to come out of the bathroom.

"What the hell was all that about? Who is that woman?" I asked Nadir.

"I don't know who she is," he answered, calmly.

"But she knew your name and our address," I said.

Nadir shrugged as if this were nothing. "Oh, she probably saw me on campus," he said. He denied knowing her entirely.

Liar, I thought to myself. I couldn't sleep the rest of the night. I didn't speak to him for days until he finally confessed, saying he had stopped seeing her when he met me. He promised me this would never happen again and that he would always remain honest and truthful with me.

Once more, I believed him. I *wanted* to believe him, and I believed in honesty between husband and wife. It didn't occur to me that anyone could be so skilled in manipulation and deceit. It also didn't occur to me that a husband would lie habitually—constantly—to his wife and think nothing of it.

I had been honest with him from the beginning. I told him that before we met, I had partied heavily at SFSU. I also told him that I had dated a few times. He said he was okay with this and assured me it was perfectly normal and acceptable in this modern era. "After all, it's 1974," he said. But every time we quarreled, he threw my past in my face.

As Nadir became more immersed in his studies, he grew more aloof, tense, and irritable. He came home progressively later each night, telling me he had to go to various libraries on campus or that he was working late at his job as a research assistant. Upon receiving his master's degree, he wanted to immediately begin working toward his PhD. "It's the only way to get a decent job in my field," he said. He suggested that he wasn't going to be able to complete his doctorate unless I helped him financially. At the same time, unbeknownst to me, Nadir was sending his parents money, money that I had earned.

Suddenly, We Had a New Islamic Household

Nadir told me he wanted us to live in an Islamic manner where the man rules the household and the woman is to obey her husband's commands. I couldn't figure out what he meant by that, at least not at first. I was quite familiar with Islamic home life since that's how I grew up. But I never recalled my father holding this belief or practice. He surely was never abusive to my mother. I also thought about my German grandmother who had converted to Islam upon marrying my grandfather. Their Islamic home didn't reflect such rules either.

Before long, it became clear that Nadir's concept of "Islamic" was radically different from mine. He demanded to know who I was talking to on the phone. If I wanted to go out somewhere on my own, he insisted on knowing where and for how long. If I was late coming home from work, he wanted to know why. When I first expressed my frustration at his need for complete control, he romanticized it by saying, "It's because I love you so" or "It's because I get worried about you."

When I was home, no matter what time of day or night, he expected me to tend to his every need, which included regular and frequent sex on demand, whenever he felt like it. He wanted his meals prepared in the Egyptian fashion, cooked and ready to eat when *he* was ready to eat. He wanted his laundry washed and his shirts and slacks ironed. He wanted the apartment clean and tidy at all times and the bathroom spotless.

Sex, meals, laundry, cleaning…He believed that all of these services were part of a wife's duty and that he was entitled to them as the husband. In short, he believed that a wife was chattel to do with as he pleased.

Whenever I refused to comply with his demands, either because I was too tired or because I wanted to do other things, we argued furiously. I was working full time, and when I told him he could do his own laundry and cleaning, it got ugly. "That's a *woman's* job," he spat. The next day he apologized and promised me once again that this behavior would not be repeated.

Before long, Nadir asked that I wear clothes that covered my arms and legs as well as a headscarf to cover my hair. He explained that this was the proper dress for Muslim women.

I thought about it and didn't like the idea one bit.

"I never had to do that under my father's roof. Why should I now?" I asked.

Nadir's face flushed red with fury, and once again I could see the vein pulsing in his temple and neck. "This is not your father's home," he said, his rage barely under control. "It's mine! You are my wife, and if you love me, you would not want me to become angry." The threat hung in the air.

I got the message, and the next day I started to wear a scarf over my hair.

I complied with Nadir's request in order to keep the peace in my marriage and because I carried a lot of guilt about my behavior before we were married—behavior that was not proper for what he called "a decent Muslim woman." He used that guilt like a weapon, flinging it at me whenever he could. He especially tried to make me feel guilty about moving in with him before we were married, even though it had been his idea. I was also afraid of what our relationship could turn into if I didn't acquiesce to his requests.

When I showed up in my headscarf at Merritt Hospital, my coworkers were baffled by the change in my appearance. I told them about the Islamic dress code my husband requested of me, then lied and said I really didn't mind. I didn't want to admit that Nadir was insisting on it.

Other demands soon followed. He didn't want me to associate with any of my friends from college or at work. He called them irrelevant lives, infidels, or negligible masses. In his world view, they were unworthy; they were nobodies.

As the weeks and months passed, these "negligible masses" came to include everyone I knew. Nadir systematically pressed me to drop all of my friends, one by one. He wanted me to socialize only with his friends' wives. "These American women are not suitable for a nice Egyptian woman like you," he'd tell me. "They're a bad influence on you."

A cactus in the rainforest, a pine tree in the desert—this time the American feminist in me rose to respond. "Bullshit! I'm an *American* woman from an *Egyptian* background!" I said and stormed out of the apartment.

Though I never mentioned my troubles at work, Norma sensed something amiss. She came by for a visit one evening. While we talked about work and giggled in the kitchen, Nadir was studying in the living room. We made sure our voices were low so he wouldn't hear us. After a few minutes, Nadir interjected himself into the conversation as if he had been part of it all along.

Nadir wasn't studying—he was eavesdropping. Norma got rattled. "This is creepy. I'm spooked," she whispered to me as she prepared to leave.

"Please don't stop coming over," I begged her. "You're the only friend I have left."

* * * * *

We'd been trying for a baby for a year, and I began to question my fertility, especially since Nadir brought it up whenever we quarreled. He hammered home his contention that Allah was punishing me for my wickedness, for not having been a "good Muslim woman" before we were married. In order for me to be cleansed, he suggested I go to the Islamic Center and have them whip me 100 times. I proposed that he lead the way for his own "cleansing."

Over time, with my self-esteem in freefall, I started to believe some of the things Nadir told me. I was extremely gullible and he knew it. Nadir was a predator and I was prey.

When I learned I was finally pregnant, I didn't get the joyous reaction from Nadir I was hoping for. Instead he became deathly still. Later that evening, with no emotion whatsoever, he informed me that he wasn't ready to be a father; he didn't want me to have this baby. I was horrified when he pressed me to get an abortion.

Soon he began yelling at me, shoving me and hitting me for continuing to refuse. The blows were initially to my arms and legs, along my back and my buttocks. Several beatings later, he progressed to my face and head. I tried to stop him but I couldn't.

Depending on what time of day it was, I'd leave the apartment and go for a walk or I'd drive to the top of the Berkeley Hills to watch the sunset. I stayed away long enough to allow him to cool down—long enough that by the time I returned home Nadir indeed was sorry, even pathetically apologetic. Sometimes he heightened the drama by getting down on his knees, crying as he begged for my forgiveness.

Entering my tenth week of pregnancy, I was still feeling nauseous. I was exhausted after a busy shift at work one day and had just vomited. When Nadir walked into the bedroom and found me resting in bed, he slowly approached, eventually looming over me, gazing at me with his icy, deep-brown eyes.

"See, if you would listen to your husband, you wouldn't be feeling this way now," he told me.

I sat up and asked, "Listen to you? We've been married three years now. I've tried to be a good wife. I speak to you in Arabic like you want me to. I'm covering my hair for the first time in my life because you want me to. I work full time to pay for our living costs and for your tuition. I clean, I cook, I do laundry, and I iron your clothes. All the while, you're constantly belittling, undermining, and badgering me, insulting my family and friends and taking me for granted! What do you mean, 'If only I would have listened to you?'"

"Yes, you are a good wife with all these things," he said, "but you didn't listen to me when I told you to get an abortion. I'm not ready to have a family."

I was livid. "You're not ready to have a family?" I wailed. "Why are you telling me this now that I'm pregnant? Why did you try to brainwash me into believing that I was not getting pregnant because I was being punished by God?"

Nadir grabbed me by the arm, dragged me from the bed to the floor, and began cursing me in Arabic. "*Ya kalba!*" he yelled. Literal translation: "You dog!" He began to kick me in my abdomen, my chest, and my back, hollering, "If you don't want to go to the doctor to get an abortion, I'll do it for you!"

Frightened he would make good on his promise, I quickly got up and tried to run to the bathroom, my safe haven. Nadir caught me before I could get there. He grabbed my arm again, shoved me into the wall, and delivered several blows to my stomach, yelling, "*Ya metnaakka! Ya bint el Kalb.*" "You're fucked! You're the daughter of a dog."

"I'll divorce you before I'd ever terminate this pregnancy!" I screamed back—in English—before my sobs overtook me. "And…I'm never wearing that damn headscarf again!"

The altercation was so loud our neighbors became concerned. One came knocking on the door. "Is everything okay?" he asked when Nadir opened the front door.

"Yes, it's fine," Nadir replied calmly. "Nothing more than a misunderstanding. You know how hysterical women can get." Nadir was a master at oozing false sincerity. After sending the neighbor on his way, Nadir apologized to me, promising me yet once more that this would never happen again.

I was embarrassed that the neighbors had heard us, but I was paralyzed by a deep-seated sense of shame and humiliation—about everything. I couldn't bring myself to tell anyone that I allowed Nadir to do this to me and to keep doing this to me.

That included my family. My parents were on holiday from Saudi Arabia shortly after this incident, and I took a few days off to go see them in Marina. My mother noticed a bruise on my arm and asked me about it. I told her I bumped into a wall. What I didn't tell her was that Nadir had pushed me into it. I was unhappy and depressed, but I was so ashamed I couldn't bear to let my family know the truth about my dismal marriage.

When I returned to Berkeley, things were a little better. Even though the verbal abuse continued, the physical violence stopped. Years later, Rick told me why. My lies had fooled no one. My parents suspected abuse when they saw me so Vati asked my brothers to go to Berkeley to have a talk with my husband. They not only talked to him, they beat the shit out of him, warning Nadir that if he continued to abuse me, they'd kill him.

And Then—Nadir's Enablers

To top off this miserable pregnancy, Nadir decided to fly his parents in for a visit. Two weeks before my due date, they arrived to stay with us in our new apartment. In anticipation of the baby's arrival, we had moved into a two-bedroom flat. Even though the timing was awful, I was eager to get to know them—at first.

Nadir's father was a little taller than Nadir, lean, and sinewy. His face was wrinkled like a raisin, and his sparse white hair made him appear older than his 68 years. Nadir's mother was 60, quite hefty with shoulder-length, jet-black hair. Her most dominant feature was her overly large brown eyes, which bulged disconcertingly out of their sockets. Her haggard, angry look was exacerbated by her prominent eyebrows, which were painted on.

Although they were wearing casual Western clothes when they first arrived, they rarely dressed this way after they settled in. Nadir's mother wore nightgowns around the house and covered her hair with a headscarf while she was at home. Oddly enough, she would take it off whenever we went out—the opposite of what Nadir was making me do. The wearing of the scarf, she explained, was to keep her hair clean when she was in the kitchen. As soon as she arrived, she took over my kitchen, which was fine with me. In my last month of pregnancy, it was a refreshing break for me to come home after a tiring day of work and not have to make dinner. She even cleaned up afterward.

Nadir's father walked with a cane, which I found puzzling because at times he seemed to be able to walk just fine on his own. Then I asked him about it.

"I can walk steadily without it, but I use it for assurance in case I lose my balance," he explained. "But most of the time, it comes in handy for this." He whacked his wife, who was seated next to him, in the legs. He said this was the best way to get her attention. They both laughed heartily afterward, but it sickened me that this woman laughed at her own abuse.

Nadir, like his brother Sammon, had learned how to treat women by watching his father. His father used the exact same language and curse words that Nadir used on me and Sammon used on Brenda. I couldn't remember one single incident between my parents that was even remotely similar to what I was witnessing between these two. My father never, ever hit my mother. Not once did I ever hear my parents speak to or about each other disrespectfully. Like all couples, they had arguments at times, but this was unlike anything I'd ever seen before.

One evening during a casual conversation, Nadir's mother asked me a puzzling question, "If the baby is a girl, would you have her circumcised?"

Confused, I thought I misunderstood her Arabic. "You mean, if it's a boy?" I replied.

"No, we would surely have a boy circumcised. There's no question about that. I'm talking about if it's a girl."

"Circumcised?" I repeated, still confused.

"Yes. Circumcision," she replied. "It's for *nadaffa*. Cleanliness. This is how women stay clean in Islam." Her matter-of-fact manner in trying to explain this made me extremely uneasy.

"Cleanliness?" I exclaimed. "If cleanliness is the issue, what's wrong with plain soap and water?"

Nadir's mother was not pleased with my frank answer and was quick to let me know it. "*Amma inti allil til adab*," she hurled at me. "My, you are rude." She glowered at me angrily then called out to Nadir that he needed to discipline his wife and instill some manners in me.

I assumed that cleanliness was a metaphor she was using for something else, but for what, I truly didn't know. Baffled, I immediately called my parents in Saudi Arabia. My mother answered the phone. I asked her if she knew anything about female *nadaffa*. She said that she would explain it to me in more detail as soon as she arrived—she was planning to be with me for the birth and to help me take care of the baby after I was discharged from the hospital.

Mutti had understood immediately that Nadir's mother meant female circumcision. She was referring to female genital mutilation, or FGM. This barbaric process involves surgical removal of all or most of the clitoris. It could also involve a partial or complete vulvectomy. Its purpose is to reduce a woman's sexual pleasure, in theory discouraging promiscuity, premarital sex, and adultery. It's neither encouraged nor condoned in Islam. In fact, there is no mention of this evil act toward females anywhere in the Holy Qur'an.

Mutti warned me, "If you have the baby before I arrive and it's a girl, don't let her out of your sight, not even for a moment!"

My confusion turned to fear and alarm.

HANNAH

One early morning in November, I went to Merritt Hospital in labor. Even though I knew most of the staff nurses, that didn't make labor any easier. And Mutti wasn't due for another week. When the contractions became more intense throughout the day, Nadir became irate with me for crying out in agony.

"*Ikhrassi ya bit,*" Nadir ordered. "Shut up, girl." I was, as he put it, "embarrassing him." *Bit* means "girl," but it's intended as an insult, not a term of endearment. A cruder but more accurate translation for the word *bit* would be "bitch" or "cunt."

"Get out of my sight!" I managed to scream at him between contractions.

Nadir stormed out of the labor room. Shortly afterwards, I received an epidural and had a Cesarean section.

The problem was I was semiconscious and all I could think of was Mutti's warning: "Never leave your baby alone for a second." My daughter was born at 6:49 p.m.

As I became more alert, I asked to see my baby. The nurses bundled her up and presented her to me. She was a beautiful, healthy, brown-eyed, brown-haired little girl—all nine pounds, two ounces of her. Her eyes were wide open, looking at the world around her. I was ecstatic at this new miracle in my arms. I looked her over to make sure that her perfect little body hadn't been tampered with.

Nadir appeared as they wheeled her into the newborn nursery and was immediately annoyed that my brother, Jerry, had arrived and had seen his baby before he did. He'd been outside smoking.

As soon as Mutti arrived, there was instant friction with Nadir's parents. The two mothers didn't get along—they disagreed about everything. My mother's assertive personality meant she didn't get along with Nadir's father either. Nadir did nothing to buffer the animosity.

Vati flew in about a week after Mutti. Being the patient, kind soul he was, my father remained calm and polite as he conversed with Nadir's parents, but he was disturbed by how this man was addressing his wife and by how he kept whacking her with his cane. "The way you use that cane is most offensive to me," Vati remarked.

"Your wife is not as acquiescent as a woman of Islam should be," Nadir's father retorted quickly. "She is too bold and aggressive." He then suggested that if my father were to make good use of a cane such as his, then perhaps his wife would be more under control.

My father eventually took me aside to ask how Nadir and his parents were treating me. I lied, of course. "Everything is fine," I said. "I can handle the situation."

Within days, there was major chaos in the apartment. My mother confronted Nadir's parents about their beliefs and attitudes, and they didn't take it well. I had already begun to resent them and asked Nadir to intervene on my behalf. I wanted him to explain to them that I was not comfortable with how they spoke to each other or to me, disregarding my opinions and feelings in my own home.

He refused, and instead he let me know that he expected me to obey his mother and father in the same unconditional way he expected me to obey him. He declared that as long as they were present in our home, they were in charge, since they were the elders.

That was not my idea of a parental visit. The tension grew, and Nadir began his ugly behavior toward me again, albeit covertly, because my parents were still with us.

I decided to have it out with him. "You're such a bigoted coward and a manipulative liar. I've had enough of your and your parents' sick, psychotic, and abusive behavior. I'm leaving you!" I shouted.

"What about my daughter? You can't just take her from me," Nadir said.

"Your daughter? Why don't you go ahead and explain to our parents under what conditions I conceived her, how I managed to carry her through all your beatings, and how supportive you were throughout my pregnancy?" I yelled, loud enough so both sets of parents could hear me. "Make sure you tell them when I was in labor how you told me, '*Ikhrassi ya bit!*' Your parents might not see this as unusual behavior but it's not going to sit well with my parents, especially with my father."

Sure enough, it didn't. As soon as my father heard these accusations, he immediately instructed me to pack my suitcase. He was taking me home to Marina until things settled down.

* * * * *

Hannah was less than two weeks old when I left Nadir and brought her to Marina. I had long discussions with Vati about some of the things that had transpired during my years of marriage to Nadir. My father was in disbelief, and he repeatedly told me that Nadir had violated the teachings of the Holy Qur'an, which emphasize the importance of mutual love and respect between spouses as well as the importance of protecting one's wife and children from harm. He read to me from Prophet Muhammed's last sermon: "…O People, it is true that you have certain rights with regard to your women, *but they also have rights over you.* Remember that you have taken them as your wives only under Allah's trust and with His permission…Do treat your women well and be kind to them, for they are your partners and committed helpers."

It was at this time that my father gave me a new Qur'an. Each chapter and verse had the original Arabic text in one column with the English translation beside it. At the bottom of each page was an interpretation of what the text meant. He encouraged me to read a little each day, emphasizing the chapters relating to women.

Vati also encouraged me to immediately formally file for separation and divorce. He galvanized some close friends to help find me a lawyer and then accompanied me to my first appointment. On January 25, 1978, National Police Day in Egypt and the third anniversary of my traditional wedding ceremony, I attended my first separation hearing. My parents had to return to Saudi Arabia a few days later, but I stayed in Marina with Hannah. I was not alone, though, because my brother John and his wife were still living there with their toddler son.

A few weeks later, Hannah and I traveled to Switzerland to visit my Tante Aidi and my grandmother, who had relocated there from Cairo a few years prior. I needed time to sort things out. I had done everything I was supposed to do. I graduated from college. I had a great job. I married a Muslim. I had been a faithful and honorable wife, and now I had a beautiful new baby. How did it all go so very wrong? My husband had turned out to be a degrading subjugator. Everything about my marriage was painful, but I knew that being in the loving environment of my grandmother and Tante Aidi would help me heal.

My grandmother, Tante Aidi, and her husband, Francis, whom I learned to call Onkel, welcomed Hannah and me with open arms. They lived in a three-story building in Ponte Tresa, a part of greater Lugano, right on the Italian-Swiss border. My grandmother lived one floor below them. Hannah and I stayed with her in her spare bedroom, which she had lovingly prepared for us, complete with a little bassinet for Hannah right next to my bed.

This was the first time I had seen Tante Aidi since my family stopped to visit en route to the US from Saudi Arabia when I was a child, and I found her to be the same energetic, confident person I remembered. She was also the same loving role model I wanted to emulate. Tante Aidi was one of the few female physicians in Europe at the time, and she was completing a mid-career residency at a local Catholic hospital, specializing in anesthesiology.

Onkel Francis was 20 years her senior. Although my parents had spoken about him many times since he and Tante Aidi married in 1967, this was the first time I'd met him. He was a tall, sturdy man with blue eyes and a corona of thinning gray hair, topped by a shiny, bald crown. His full name was Francis Bott, and he was an artist of some renown. He proudly showed me various collections of his abstract artwork and told me about his largest stained-glass project, a commission from the Rothschild family.

I stayed in Lugano for six weeks and spoke only German during that time. Each day, I silently thanked my mother for her insistence that I retain and practice it every day. I spent a lot of time talking with my grandmother, just as I had as a child in Cairo. Her gentle nature was now tinged with sadness. She never quite got over the death of her husband and then of her son, my Onkel Rolf.

A few days after my arrival in Switzerland, Nadir called. He apologized profusely and asked me to come back to him. He promised me that things would change if I returned.

"Just one more chance," he begged.

I wasn't buying it. "I am tired of your abusive behavior, and I don't trust you to keep your word," I told him. Then I hung up.

After that he called daily, pleading with me to come back to him, saying how he couldn't live without me. He told me his parents had gone to stay with his brother in Delaware so I wouldn't have to deal with them anymore. He also told me that one of his Egyptian friends at Berkeley had recently committed suicide because his wife had thrown him out of the house after she discovered he was cheating on her. He had ingested cyanide he pilfered from the lab where he studied.

Nadir then deployed the ultimate weapon—guilt—and suggested that if I didn't come back to him, he might do the same thing. It was a no-win situation. If I left him and he did commit suicide, I would feel partially responsible and carry the burden of his death for the rest of my life. On the other hand, if I returned to him and gave him one more chance, what were the odds that he would continue with his abusive behavior? Maybe, just maybe, I told myself, he had finally learned his lesson. I desperately wanted that to be true.

After agonizing over what to do, I, in my heart and idealistic mind, decided to return to Nadir, and I called my parents in Saudi Arabia to let them know.

"I brought you to *Amreeka* so you can have an education, so you could have control of your destiny—and you go backwards on me?" my father asked. Vati sounded extremely disappointed in my decision, and I could sense his sadness and his concern for Hannah and me.

"I feel sorry for Nadir, and I think he will truly change his ways. Besides, I want to give him a chance to experience fatherhood," I explained.

"He'll never change!" my father insisted. I could hear the pain and anguish in his cracking voice as he tried to make me understand. He added, "But if that's your decision, your mother and I will support you. May Allah be with you and protect you, *ya habibti.*"

And things did change for the better until I made the mistake of assuming Nadir would take on new fatherhood. Instead I became a single parent because Nadir didn't participate in any of Hannah's care. I read to her and played with her. I took her for swimming lessons. These should have been family activities but Nadir wasn't interested. He remained utterly focused on his studies. He also continued to smoke at home, leaving dirty ashtrays all over the apartment. When Hannah was beginning to walk, I found her putting cigarette ashes into her mouth, and I went ballistic. Nadir didn't flinch. He didn't celebrate her first steps or her first words. He remained entirely detached from fatherhood and avoided having anything to do with his daughter.

CHAPTER 8

WHERE IS INDIANA?

Nadir got his PhD, and after refusing several entry-level job offers, he finally accepted a position with a company that produced nickel and cobalt-based alloys. The firm was located in Kokomo, an industrial and manufacturing city in Indiana, roughly 60 miles north of Indianapolis.

We drove across the country in our new green Mustang. Hannah was 16 months old and I was in my third month of pregnancy with our second child. Nadir's attitude had improved once I returned to him. He still had a temper but for Hannah to have a father I could handle his anger. Nadir was frustrated by the frequent stops a toddler and a pregnant woman had to make along the way. Above all, he wasn't happy about my second pregnancy.

Over the next few months, once we purchased a home and settled in, life started to normalize. I liked the community, and as I got to know my neighbors, I liked it even more. A retired couple, Sarah and Lawrie, lived next door. It was immediately evident that they were from Scotland: Although they had come to America some 30 years earlier, they still spoke with a heavy Scottish burr. Sarah's warm smile and gentle composure emanated motherly love. Lawrie was a tall, thin but rugged man with a thick head of white hair and a gruff-but-endearing presence. The more I interacted with them, the more I liked them. But Nadir wanted nothing to do with them.

Early in our marriage, I had worked full time to pay for our living expenses and for Nadir's tuition. Now pregnant with our second child and chasing around a toddler, I made the decision to stay home. As much as this is a normal decision in most households, for me this was a mistake that put me at the whim of a twisted, control freak and I almost lost myself. As soon as Nadir started working full time, he let me know that this was his one and only job. He was the breadwinner and because he was the one leaving early for work and coming home tired in the evening, all he wanted to do was put his feet up and relax when he came home. Since I was home all day, it was up to me to take care of everything else. In addition to the routine housecleaning, laundry, grocery shopping, cooking, and childcare, Nadir also expected me to do the yard work and take care of the swimming pool. In the winter when it snowed, I was to shovel the snow and clear the driveway so he could leave for work. I tried to keep up with everything but it was tiring, especially toward the end of my pregnancy.

On a late July evening, I was resting in bed when Nadir came home from work. He became furious when I told him I didn't have dinner prepared. It was toward the end of my pregnancy, his behavior had been gradually reverting, and I was exhausted. "*Ya kalba, ya hamarra!*" he shouted. "You bitch, you donkey!"

"Make your own damn dinner," I cried.

"Nothing is getting done around here," he bellowed. "You've become useless and good for nothing, lying around all day."

"I'm in my last month of pregnancy, you heartless imbecile. Can't you have even an ounce of compassion?" I retorted.

The argument frightened Hannah, who began to cry. Rather than comforting her, Nadir left the house. When I picked her up, I was crying as hard as she was. I felt her little body quivering as she whimpered and sobbed. I took her into bed with me, rocking her in my arms to soothe her fears and calm mine.

Nadir didn't return home until late that night. He didn't tell me where he'd been, and I didn't ask. I lay in bed with Hannah at my side as I felt my unborn child tumbling and kicking inside me. I wondered whether the baby was frightened by the arguments or could sense my sadness and despair. After I placed Hannah into her crib, I went downstairs to sleep on the couch and remained there until Nadir left for work the next morning. When he came home that evening, I had dinner ready for him, but I had neither the appetite to eat with him nor the desire to sit with him at the table. True to form, a few days later Nadir calmed down and apologized for his behavior, promising once more that this would never happen again. *Yeah, sure,* I thought to myself.

Soon afterwards, Nadir brought up the subject of having his parents come for another visit. Remembering what happened when Hannah was born, I made it clear that I didn't want a repeat scenario. I didn't want them to arrive until *after* I fully recovered from childbirth.

"Besides," I added, "Mutti is coming to stay with us for a couple of weeks. She'll be taking care of Hannah while I'm at the hospital and you're at work." Nadir said nothing, but I sensed he was not looking forward to her arrival.

Amal

Giving birth this time was a little more controlled. Because I was prescheduled for a C-section, I wouldn't have to experience labor contractions. "This time it will be a boy! I just know it!" Nadir announced before my due date. "And his name will be Omar!"

"You sound so confident the baby will be a boy. What if it's a girl?" I replied. Nadir didn't respond.

Mutti arrived a few days before my C-section to help with the chores and to begin caring for Hannah. She slept on the twin bed in Hannah's room since Hannah was still sleeping in her crib. I had placed a bassinette next to my bed, ready for the arrival of the new baby.

"It's a girl!" The nurses swaddled her and handed her to me to hold. She was alert and looked straight into my eyes. *Another girl, another sweet little girl*, I thought. Oh, the blessings of God. I began to cry—tears of joy at being blessed with two beautiful, healthy little girls. I'd always wanted a sister. I now had two little girls instead, to love and raise the best way I could. I was so grateful! *Alhamdulillah!*

Nadir wasn't allowed into the operating room for the C-section. He sat in the fathers' lounge as was customary in those days, nervously awaiting the news. When he heard that we had another daughter, he sulked. Rather than being elated for the birth of a beautiful, healthy baby, he wallowed in the disappointment that it wasn't a son.

But that wasn't the worst of it. While I was in the recovery room, Nadir stood at my bedside and commented on how light-skinned the baby was and that she had blonde hair. "She doesn't resemble me at all," he said.

The insinuation that this was not his child was left hanging in the air. I felt a surge of anxiety but I was still groggy from the anesthesia. I let the drugs take over and allowed myself to go within. The teardrops burned my face as they trickled from the outer corners of my eyes.

That evening, Nadir, my mother, and Hannah came to visit me. Hannah was bubbly with anticipation. She wanted to see her baby sister, who was sleeping peacefully in the crib next to my bed. She wasn't named yet because Nadir had been sure the baby would be a boy. I had a name in mind, though. A beautiful name…Amal.

"How about if we named baby sister Amal?" I asked Hannah while looking at Nadir for a response.

"Yes, Mommy, baby Amal," Hannah replied gleefully. My mother picked up the baby and showed her to Hannah, who was excited and eager to touch her.

"That sounds like a beautiful name, don't you think so, Nadir?" my mother commented.

Although physically present, Nadir wasn't really there. "Name her whatever you want," he muttered as he turned away. Nadir chose not to touch his newborn daughter, pick her up, or interact with her in any way.

The next day, he came to see me at the hospital immediately after work. Without pretense or preamble, he made his prior insinuation explicit. He declared that this baby was not his. Her skin was too pale, she had blonde hair, and her facial features didn't resemble him in any way whatsoever.

"Are you implying that she is another man's child? That I slept with another man?" I asked.

"Did you?" he asked flatly. His tone was impassive and detached, like a police detective with a prime suspect.

"Of course not, you cruel, heartless prick!" I wailed.

Nadir said nothing, did nothing. "Get out of my room! Get out!" I shouted. My cries caught the attention of the nurses, who immediately responded and asked what the problem was.

"Get him out of here!" I screamed.

Nadir shrugged. "I don't know what's wrong with her," he said glibly. "She gets so emotional about everything." It was the same smarmy, nonchalant tone he used to get rid of the neighbor at the door in Berkeley after he'd been punching me in the stomach.

And I felt about the same way—as if I'd been struck in the gut. I cried inconsolably, devastated by his accusation. Twice now, Nadir had stolen the pure joy of childbirth from me. His callous indifference and emotional cruelty had turned new motherhood into abject despair.

The following day, Nadir unexpectedly walked into my room. It was noon. "You must come home today—now!" he told me. "I refuse to spend another evening alone with your mother. She's Hitler!" What he meant was that my mother was a strong woman who didn't put up with his bullshit.

"I can't—it's only my second postoperative day," I replied. I was getting out of bed and walking a bit, but the incision still hurt like crazy and I was taking pain pills every four hours.

"You must tell your doctor that you need to go home now," he demanded.

"They won't release me. It's much too soon. The incision hasn't yet begun to heal. Besides, we haven't officially named our daughter or completed the birth certificate."

My doctor refused to release me. In the interest of preserving the peace in my household, I signed myself out of the hospital against medical advice. The nurses gave me a form to fill out and instructed me to send it to the health department within 10 days with the baby's official legal name.

Thankfully, my father arrived in Kokomo a few days later. He was in his usual jovial mood and happy to meet his new granddaughter, but his joy quickly evaporated. Mutti filled him in on Nadir's surly behavior toward me as well as his complete indifference to his daughters. I teared up looking at my father—there was a profound sadness in his eyes, and his furrowed brow betrayed how worried he was for my wellbeing. I knew that both of my parents suspected that Nadir was mistreating me, but I still wouldn't dare tell them how bad things really were.

As soon as Nadir came home from work that evening, my father immediately had a private conversation with him. Neither of them ever told me what was said, but Nadir's behavior improved dramatically, at least until my parents left a few days later to return to their home.

* * * * *

Nadir's letters to and from his parents continued regularly. I assumed he was inviting them to Kokomo for a visit because we had discussed the matter before Amal was born. He just never told me when. Then one evening in October, Nadir announced that his parents were arriving—the next day.

"Tomorrow?" I asked. "Why didn't you tell me sooner so I could prepare for their arrival?" I asked.

I screamed at him that I wasn't ready to have them around and that there wasn't enough time to prepare. Amal wasn't even two months old yet.

Nadir set his beer bottle on the table, walked over to me, grabbed me by my left arm, and shook me. "Don't you dare speak to me like that! Especially not in front of my parents!" he threatened. Then he threw me to the floor, kicking me in the lower back and buttocks area several times, shouting, "*Ya kalba! Ya kalba!*" This was his favorite putdown for me. This episode happened in full view of the children, who began wailing in fright.

I managed to pull myself off the floor. I picked up Amal, grabbed Hannah's hand, and took them upstairs as fast as I could. After putting the girls to bed, I wept silently. By now I had mastered the art of crying without making a sound. Then I began to pray. "What have I done to deserve this, oh Allah? Please help me, God. Please have mercy on me, oh Lord. I have to stay strong for my daughters. I have to stay strong for Hannah and Amal. I'm all they have."

NADIR'S PARENTS: ROUND TWO

The arrival of Nadir's parents was congenial. After the usual greetings and small talk, they settled in. As soon as they changed into their comfortable clothes, Nadir's mother announced to me that I was to call her *Um Dr. Nadir, el mouhandis*, meaning "mother of Dr. Nadir, the engineer." Her husband was to be addressed as *Abo Dr. Nadir, el mouhandis*: "Father of Dr. Nadir, the engineer."

"Sure whatever," I mumbled under my breath.

Nadir decided that his parents would stay in the family room, and I agreed because we didn't have an extra bedroom. I kept myself busy with the girls as I watched him grudgingly pull out two rollaway cots from storage and set them up in the furthest corner of the family room.

A few weeks after their arrival, I told Nadir and his parents that I intended to start working again, at least part time. I wanted to keep up my nursing skills, but I also needed to get away from my tormentor and his parents. Nadir kept saying "no," but I was persistent in telling him that I needed this professional stimulation. "What professional stimulation? You're just a nurse. In Egypt, they're called *khadamma*, 'maid!' And I won't have my wife working in that type of job," Nadir declared, holding his head up high and proud.

"Well, we're not in Egypt, we're in America," I countered. "And besides," I added, "*khadamma* or not, my nursing job was good enough to pay for your graduate school tuition and our living expenses—not to mention your parents' flights from Egypt!"

Nadir's father then spoke to his son as if I weren't there. "She's exactly like her mother," he said. "Talking to her husband disrespectfully like that. You should not accept that, Nadir."

He then turned to me. "Don't be so upset," he told me. "Nadir is a good man who will provide for his family, so there's no need for you to work. It wouldn't be good for the children if you leave them. They need their mother at home. You should take care of them properly, and you must take care of your husband in a respectful manner." He went on and on, sounding like an old uneducated tribal chief spouting off a myriad of archaic reasons I had to stay home, punctuating each "irrefutable" point he made by gesturing with his cane, as if it were a pointer in a classroom and I was the insubordinate student.

I became more determined than ever to go back to work. In late November, I received my Indiana RN license and accepted a job at Howard Community Hospital as a staff nurse in the obstetrics department. OB was a new specialty for me, and I came to enjoy it. Nadir was not happy that I defied him, but I remained steadfast and told him I hadn't gone to college to stay home to serve him and cater to all his needs. His expression clouded. He was, I thought, resisting the urge to hit me in front of his parents.

Working as an OB nurse required rotations on the labor and delivery deck, as well as the postpartum and the newborn nursery unit. It was challenging, exciting work, and I felt better almost immediately. As I polished my skills, my long-buried self-confidence resurfaced. As an added plus, I was earning my own money once more.

I worked the night shift, 11:00 p.m. to 7:00 a.m., two to three nights a week, leaving Nadir with his parents and the girls. As soon as my shift ended, I rushed home to find the kids already awake. I was not surprised to see that it was Nadir's mother who tended to the girls and started their day as Nadir and his father waited to have their breakfast served.

Although we are Muslims and celebrate Islamic holidays, we continued to celebrate Christmas as a beautiful fun season, complete with a tree. Nadir's parents believed this to be shameful behavior and *haram* as a Muslim and told Nadir how they felt. And I didn't care how they felt about it. Soon it was February, and Nadir's parents were still with us. They had overstayed their welcome. I was tired of Nadir's father sitting around the house all day, doing nothing. He had no interaction with his grandchildren whatsoever—like father, like son. He moved from couch to chair to couch, all the while blathering about unimportant things that he and Nadir's mother did back in Egypt. He talked to his wife and about his wife in a terribly disrespectful way. They bickered back and forth in Arabic all day long, usually in front of my daughters. He also ordered his wife to get him this or that and used his cane to reinforce his commands whenever he felt it was necessary. Nadir's mother shouted and cursed at him but did what she was told. I felt a little sorry for her—I believed she was a victim of this sick, radical, misogynistic family.

On a brighter side and to Nadir's mother's credit, she cooked a delicious Egyptian dinner every night. I let her do whatever she wanted in the kitchen because that gave me more time to spend with my babies. "Nadir is my favorite son," she told me one day. "He takes good care of us. He sends us money when we need it. Not like Sammon. Sammon is selfish. He doesn't write much or send us any money. He forgets that we are his parents and that we raised him," she complained.

It was surprising enough to learn that we were supporting them, but to my astonishment, she continued. "But at least Sammon isn't asking *us* for money like the nasty little bastard children back in Egypt. They're always coming to our apartment, begging for food or money. They pester us all the time."

"What beggars? What nasty children are you talking about?" I asked.

"His," she replied as she pointed toward her husband. "I'm sick of having them come to us, begging for food, clothes, and money," she added.

My jaw dropped. "You have other children?" I asked Nadir's father.

"Yes. They're such a nuisance, coming to us almost daily, asking for anything they can get, the little beggar bastards." He said this matter-of-factly, as if it were another casual topic of conversation. "I don't even know how many there are—it seems there are different ones coming on different days. They're just poor little bastards," he said scornfully. "Their mothers are *sharmutas* [whores]. Sometimes they come around begging too, always wanting something from me. I tell them all to scram and leave, but they keep coming back."

He turned angrily to his wife, who was sitting next to him on the couch. "Why did you have to bring them up now, *ya hamarra*—you ass!" he demanded. Then struck her across the shins with his cane.

I couldn't believe what I'd heard. Nadir's father had sired other children with different women he wasn't married to, didn't know how many exactly, and called each mother of those children a whore! I looked at him with utter disgust. *If they're whores,* I thought to myself, *what does that make you, Abo Dr. Nadir, el mouhandis?*

Sickened by what I was hearing, it was time to confront Nadir about his parents leaving our home.

"When are your parents leaving?"

"When they're ready to leave!" Nadir replied.

"They were supposed to be gone right after Christmas. It's now May and they're still here!" I shot back.

Nadir rushed at me and forcefully grabbed my arm. He snarled, "*Ikhrassi ya bit!*" just softly enough that his parents wouldn't hear him.

I was intimidated. But I insisted again, "When are your parents leaving?"

"They're not yet ready to leave! And keep your voice down!" he barked. He didn't want his parents to hear that I was talking to him loudly, as if I were scolding him.

I was tired of all the excuses, and after months of getting the runaround from Nadir, I finally confronted them directly. "When are you returning to Egypt?" I asked with the full force of resentment in my voice.

"Are you trying to rush us?" Nadir's father responded, as if this was somehow the strangest question I could ask. I turned to Nadir.

"If you don't get your parents out of here and on a flight home as soon as possible, I will leave you!" I said.

Nadir smirked, trying to pretend to his parents that he had the situation under control. Then he went to the kitchen, got a beer, and plopped himself on the couch. He completely ignored me.

After waiting several minutes for a response and not getting one, I picked up the phone and called Nadir's brother Sammon in Delaware.

"Alloh," he said.

"You and Nadir have 48 hours to figure out how to get your parents out of my house. Otherwise, I will call the police and have them physically removed!" I shouted.

Sammon tried to placate me, talking down to me in a condescending tone that made me even angrier than I already was. "Two days," I spat. "If you and Nadir don't make arrangements to get your parents out of my house within 48 hours, I will call the police and have them taken out!"

At that point, Nadir grabbed the phone to talk to his brother. I don't remember the details of their conversation but I did hear Nadir discussing airline reservations.

Two days later, I saw Nadir's parents packing their bags and grumbling. Nadir took them to the airport and sent them off to Sammon's house in Delaware. I felt sorry for Brenda, who would have to deal with them, but as much as I was sad for her, I was happier for myself.

Days later, Nadir began receiving regular letters from his parents. At first, they came from Delaware but within a month, they bore an Egyptian postmark and return address. The letters also seemed to be coming more frequently.

In the wake of so much upheaval, I tried to keep up some kind of normal routine for the girls. I kept my part-time nursing job after his parents left while Hannah continued going to Montessori school.

A month later Vati was diagnosed with end stage renal disease (ESRD). He'd had flu-like symptoms when I had Amal but now his kidneys were failing and there was no cure.

My brothers and I organized a family reunion in Petersburg, Virginia near Vati's new assignment in Fort Lee so we could all be there for family support. All my brothers and their families attended. Nadir declined to go saying that he had too much work to do. But we all knew that Nadir not only didn't want to go—he didn't want me going either. "You're my wife, and you are supposed to be with me, your husband!" he said.

"My father is ill. No one can say how many days, months, or years he has left. I'm going, and I'm taking the girls with me."

The conversation quickly mushroomed into a heated argument, but I stood my ground. Even after I had bathed the girls and put them to bed, Nadir kept pressing me not to go. When that didn't persuade me, he told me he wanted to make love.

"Make love? Are you kidding me? I don't love you!"

Nadir slapped me so hard that I almost fell to the floor. He then grabbed me by the arm and threw me on the bed. "I'm your husband, and you will do as I say!" he growled.

Within seconds, I found myself pinned down. Nadir then proceeded to rape me. The force of his penetration caused a painful perineal tear, and I bled for days. As bad as the physical pain was, however, the emotional pain was worse. I felt violated, completely alone, and vulnerable. This was my husband, the man who was supposed to love and protect me, but instead, he was the one I most needed protection from. I was so ashamed of myself and of what my life had become...and I was too embarrassed to seek medical care for the perineal tear.

The next morning, I made flight arrangements for Petersburg. When Nadir came home after work and saw me packing, he apologized profusely for what he had done the previous night. He had gifts in hand for me and for Hannah and Amal. Pretty little dresses for the girls and a beautiful Concord watch for me.

"I'm so sorry about last night. I didn't mean to hurt you. Please forgive me. I'll never do that again. Please don't go to Virginia with the girls," he pleaded.

What a manipulative bastard. How sick, how conniving was he, trying to buy me off with gifts and empty promises.

I began to cry again as I continued packing. "I should've called the police last night, you prick!" I said.

"You're my wife!" Nadir reminded me. "You can't call the police because you're my wife!" What he meant was that as his wife, I was his property to do with as he wished. That was his distorted interpretation of our faith, one he inherited from his father.

"I won't be your wife for much longer! I want a divorce!" I retorted.

"You want a divorce? Go get one!" he shouted. "You're used up. You're like used furniture. No one will want you because you've been fucked! You'll be alone for the rest of your life."

Being alone sounded so much better than being with him.

"And as for the children, I'll see to it that you never see them again," he said, as he went to the kitchen.

This, on the other hand, really scared me. I immediately thought about Samir, one of Nadir's colleagues in Berkeley, who was married to an American woman. Like Nadir, he was abrasive, rude, controlling, self-centered, and horribly abusive to his wife. He often insulted her openly in front of their friends and children. They had five children together, but after receiving his US citizenship and his graduate degree, Samir took four of them to Egypt when she filed for divorce. He left the fifth child behind in California with his ex-wife because the boy was severely disabled. As far as I knew, she never saw Samir or any of her other children again.

Less than a minute later, Nadir came back, beer in hand, and apologized, rationalizing his behavior and making excuses for it. I tuned him out. There was nothing left to say.

Our Family Reunion

My father had often told me that what he loved most in life was to be surrounded by his children and grandchildren. Now he beamed proudly when he saw all of us together. True to form, my mother seemed unaffected, even though her own mother was visiting from Switzerland. If Mutti was moved by the gathering, she never voiced it out loud, at least not to me.

The children were all so cute and played with each other while we adults caught up with what had happened since the last time we were together. Rick was busy with his medical residency and was raising three children with his wife, Barbara. John lived in

California and worked as a banking officer. He and his wife had two children. Jerry and Ralph, still young bachelors, were students, one at university and the other at the police academy. One of the most beautiful events of that visit was that we were able to have a professional family photograph taken of the entire family together, exactly as my father had wanted.

But part of me was secretly in despair, about both my father's health and about the wreckage of my marriage. When I arrived at my parents' home, I didn't say anything to them about what had happened in Kokomo. I didn't want my situation to cast a pall over the reunion. All I said was that Nadir and his parents were not pleased that I had insisted they leave in May.

In a quiet moment alone with Vati, I mentioned the growing volume of correspondence between Nadir and his parents. "Ever since they left, Nadir seems to be getting more letters than usual from them, and I've noticed that he is writing back to them just as frequently."

"Do you know what's in the letters?" my father asked.

"No. They're all in Arabic." Although I still understood and spoke fluent Arabic, I hadn't retained my Arabic reading and writing skills.

"When you get back to Kokomo, send me some of them so I can translate them for you," my father said. "I want to know what these *balady* people are up to." I giggled: *Balady* in Arabic means "hillbilly," "hayseed," or "redneck."

"I will, but if Nadir finds out I'm spying on him, he'll be angry with me," I said. By now, I was terrified of what Nadir could do when he got angry.

"Send me a few at a time. I'll translate them and send them back to you with the translations. When you receive them, send me a few more, and a few more after that. Nadir is so self-absorbed, he won't even notice," my father said.

"I'll ask my neighbors, Sarah and Lawrie, if you can send the letters and translations to *their* house," I said. "That way there won't be any chance that Nadir will check the mail before I do."

RETURN TO KOKOMO

After returning to Indiana, I immediately collected a few of Nadir's parents' letters and sent them off to Vati. Sarah called to let me know when the return batch arrived. I promptly started reading my father's translations. Nadir's parents had written at length about how rude I was, "like her mother...doesn't know how to respect her husband in his abode...is teaching the children things that are *haram*," by which they meant the celebration of Christmas. No mention of how I was doing or how the girls were.

I put the originals back in their place on Nadir's desk, then gathered up the next batch and sent them off to Vati. My father soon called to say how disturbed he was about what the letters contained. "To sum it all up, *ya habibti*," my father said softly, his voice quivering as he spoke, "Nadir used you as a steppingstone to acquire his green card and to become a US citizen."

It all made sense. I could see the pattern: Nadir's abusive behavior had escalated in a series of steps, each of them punctuated by an event on the path to citizenship. He became arrogant and offensive as soon as we married and got more vicious after he acquired his green card. Finally, he became truly brutal after he became a US citizen. And he neither cared about nor wanted to be tied down to his two daughters. How had I not picked up on this earlier? The signs were all around me, and I just didn't see them. I was anguished by the overwhelming shame of my naïveté.

Crying became a daily part of my routine. I took Amal and Hannah to the park and wept silently as I pushed them on the swings. My daughters were the only good thing to come out of this miserable marriage. My mind spun constantly as I thought about the years I'd spent with Nadir—the lost years. I thought about how hard I'd worked to pay for his graduate school tuition and our daily living expenses. I thought about his escalating mental and physical abuse and his systematic demolition of my self-esteem. I contemplated the many blatant infidelities Nadir had committed over the years—vehemently lying and denying them, defending himself before he finally admitted to them, apologizing and promising he wouldn't continue this behavior. Each time, I believed him and forgave him. It was a perfect dance.

I reflected on how desperately Nadir had wanted to accept one of the overseas job offers he'd received and how he had tried to coerce me into leaving the country with him to live in Libya. As mortified as I was for having stayed in this wretched relationship for so long, I reluctantly gave myself a little credit for not doing that. Thanks to Allah and my father's strong warning, I was grateful that at least I'd had the courage and fortitude to stand my ground and stay in America.

Day after day, I continued my routines with the children and my part-time job. I was taking care of my daughters and putting one foot in front of the other, all the while pondering how I'd gotten to this pathetic point in my life.

The Humiliating and Last Straw

One day, I went upstairs with the girls and found toys scattered all over the floor. I asked Hannah to pick them up and put them away. And that's when it happened, the moment that would be another turning point in my life.

"*Ikhrassi Mommy. Ikhrassi ya bit*," Hannah said. Having listened to Nadir saying this to me almost daily, she repeated what she had heard.

"Don't ever say that to Mommy again, sweetheart," I told her, as firmly and as gently as I could. "That's very hurtful."

"Sorry, Mommy," she replied sheepishly.

Nadir had wanted no part of teaching his daughters but they were learning from him just the same. And what they were learning was that I was a punching bag, a handy target for insults and scorn. This was the absolute last straw for me, and I resolved then and there to do whatever it took to get not only myself out of that hell but my daughters too.

The next day, Sarah called to tell me that the last batch of letters from my father had arrived. As I read them, I realized that I was out of time. Nadir's father had written that they'd convinced a good friend of theirs to marry off his daughter to Nadir. They said she was a beautiful young *anessa*, or "gentle miss," who was educated and came from a good family. Nadir's parents assured him that he would be so much happier with a *real* Egyptian wife—how soon could he fly to Cairo to meet her? His father also offered advice on how to seize all our assets before he left. He wanted to make sure that the girls and I were left with nothing…like his "bastard" children and their *sharmuta* mothers back in Egypt.

Without hesitation, I opened the yellow pages and found a lawyer who could see me first thing the next morning. With his help, I filed for divorce and for a restraining order. Nadir would be served at work that same afternoon. I shut down our joint credit cards and withdrew most of the money from the joint checking account. I returned home from the bank in time to meet the locksmith who changed all the locks to the house, including the garage door opener.

It was a pretty safe bet that Nadir would try to flee the country to avoid paying alimony or child support, so I collected what I knew were his most valuable items, including his American passport—*especially* his American passport. I also grabbed his birth certificate, his degrees and diplomas, his precious Egyptian music albums, and the most damning letters from his parents. Then I took them next door to Sarah and Lawrie for safekeeping. After that, there was nothing to do but wait for him to come home.

The scene played out as I expected it would with Nadir becoming outraged when he found himself locked out. "Let me in. Let me in. This is my house. I need to talk to you. Please let me in." Nadir kept yelling as he pounded on the door.

He was making such a racket that all our neighbors heard him. Several of them came out of their houses wondering what all the commotion was about. Eventually one of them called the police. When they arrived, Nadir was still beating his fists on the door, alternately demanding and pleading to be let in.

I showed the officers the restraining order and told them that Nadir had been served with a copy of it earlier in the day. I also said that I feared for my safety and the safety of the children.

"You can't keep me out of my house! This is my house! I live here!" Nadir shrieked.

"Did you receive a restraining order today, sir?" one of the officers asked him.

"Yes, but this is my house!" he ranted. "I live here! Where am I supposed to go?"

"You'll have to take that up with the court, sir. With this restraining order, you cannot be here. You need to leave now," the other officer explained.

"She can't do this," he insisted.

Yes, I can, I said to myself. *And I did!*

But I resisted the urge to say anything out loud, realizing it was far better to let the court order and the policemen do the talking for me. The look on Nadir's face was priceless—the crux of it was that despite the law, despite the restraining order, he couldn't believe this was happening to him. There was a simple reason why—

he didn't believe that women were entitled to any rights whatsoever. He couldn't comprehend that *he* was the one who had to
vacate the premises. And he was actually astonished that the police
officers were making him leave.

"Where am I supposed to go? I don't even have my things!"
Nadir whined.

"You need to find a place, anyplace but here. Just as the restraining order states, sir," the first officer told Nadir firmly.

"But my things! I need my things!" Nadir insisted.

"What things, sir?" The two officers were becoming irritated
with him.

"My clothes and other...ah...ah...things," Nadir replied vague-
ly. He didn't want to mention them in front of me but I knew
exactly what things he meant. I also knew he wasn't going to find
them. These were the items I'd taken next door.

"Okay," I said. "If one of you officers will accompany him, I'll
allow him to come inside to collect his clothes and whatever else
he wants. Then please escort him out and away from here."

Nadir looked at me with puppy-dog eyes. He pleaded with me
once again to forgive him but I'd fallen for that pitiful look all
too often. "Save it for the judge!" I said, gesturing to the officers
to allow him in to pack a bag. He grabbed a suitcase and filled it
with his clothes. Then he rummaged through the house, frantical-
ly looking for the items I'd stashed next door. He left, of course,
without finding them.

The girls were understandably upset at all the noise and ruck-
us. Hannah was clinging to my leg and Amal was in my arms,
her head buried in my shoulder. Their father didn't bother to say
goodbye to them when he left.

After the officers escorted Nadir out, I locked the door and
breathed a huge sigh of relief. At last, I felt safe and without a

doubt, I was treated as an equal human being. After calming the girls down, I bathed them and put them to bed.

Vati was overjoyed when I told him the news. "Finally!" he declared. "This time you must stay with it until your divorce is finalized. No more chances for that egotistical, self-absorbed dirty *kalb!*" My father didn't usually swear. For him to call Nadir a dog was saying a lot.

"There's no way in hell I'll ever back down again," I said. "Thank you so much for translating all those letters for me."

"*Alhamdulillah* that I could do it for you, *ya habibti*. Now we know how devious he really is, and by having this knowledge, you'll be able to protect yourself and your own darling daughters. Make sure you remain steadfast and be vigilant wherever you go," he said, before hanging up.

I was afraid of what Nadir might do in the event he figured out how to get in. For the next several months, sleeping with a hatchet under my pillow became a new normal. My brother, Jerry, was on quarter break from university and came to stay with the girls and me for added support.

DIVORCE

I filed for divorce in October 1980. Our first hearing occurred three weeks later. The process was long and drawn-out, primarily because Nadir objected to everything, but it was all for naught. The state of Indiana understood what he never did—that under the law, I was his equal, not his property. *Alhamdulillah!*

This made him mad—about everything. Nadir was angry at the system for allowing the divorce to go through and for ordering him to pay all attorneys' fees, including mine. He was angry that I received sole custody of the girls and that he was allotted a four-week summer visitation each year.

Above all, he was irate about the court-ordered child support he was obligated to pay and was stunned to discover that he couldn't get out of it. Failure to pay would result in income confiscation or even jail time.

Furious with me and the legal system, Nadir began to lash out. He threatened to take the girls to Libya, vowing once more that I'd never see them again. I immediately alerted the court and applied for social security numbers for the girls. I knew this was essential to keeping my daughters safe. Accordingly, I hid the cards where Nadir couldn't get to them. He may have threatened to kidnap them to Libya but it would be impossible to apply for passports and take them out of the country without knowing their social security numbers.

The worst of it was that I knew he didn't really want custody of the girls at all. He didn't even want to pay for their food and clothing or maintenance. He was merely using them as a weapon against me because he knew they were the most important priority in my life.

My divorce was final on April 8, 1981, and it was music to my ears. I was finally free from this nightmare of a marriage. I was finally free from this tyrant who had nearly choked the life out of me—literally and figuratively—for years. I was finally free to be a mom to my daughters and focus on my career as a nurse. I felt as if I'd been given another chance at life. I felt like I could breathe again.

But now what? In high school, I had wanted to be an airline pilot. After graduating from college, I had contemplated joining the Air Force as a nurse. My father knew that I wanted to travel and that I had a sense of adventure. Perhaps, now was the time, he suggested, to revisit the possibility of becoming an Air Force nurse. I called the recruiting office at Grissom Air Force Base, only

12 miles from Kokomo. They told me they would send me paperwork but after several weeks, nothing had arrived.

Too slow, I decided. I wanted to do something with my life now—to finally be respected and be treated as an equal. I contacted the local Army recruiting office for information. They responded immediately and enthusiastically. Within days, I welcomed a recruiter into my home to discuss the possibility of an Army career. They really wanted me to join, and I was excited about the possibilities of both travel and advancement. Finally, I knew what the next chapter of my life would be: I would become an officer in the US Army Nurse Corps. This seemed to be what I need to be respected and feel like an equal human being.

*Vati and President Mohamed Naguib holding my brother Tarek
1953*

My 3 brothers - Tarek carrying Sherief, Hazem and me in Saudi Arabia 1960

Me carrying baby Ralph 1962

Our Family Celebrating Christmas 1962 at Leona's House (L to R - Me, Tarek, Hazem, Vati, Baby Ralph, Mutti and Sherief

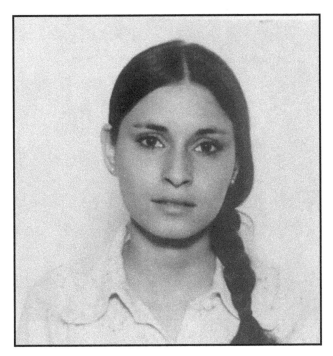

My passport photo 1975

My Daughters at home in Wheaton, MD Nov 1981

My Parents and Daughters while I was at Ft. Bragg, NC July 1983

Promotion to Major at Ft. Meade, MD. My Commander to my right and Vati to my left - 1985

97th General Hospital Compound - Frankfurt, W. Germany

Our Wedding in Nykobing-Falster, Denmark - June 1990

The OB/GYN 'Crew' with Chief Nurse, Colonel Nancy Adams - 97th General Hospital, Frankfurt, W. Germany — 1990

Promotion to Lt. Colonel, Ft. Belvoir, VA - General Adams to my right and Phil to my left – Jan. 1994

Ft. Belvoir, VA – Dec. 1995

Holding Baby Casey at Camp Casey, S. Korea – July 1999

Ready to board Medevac Helicopter, Camp Casey, S. Korea - 1999

ANC Centennial Cake #1 for Walter Reed Army Medical Center Celebration – Feb. 2001

ANC Centennial Cake #2 for the Greater DC Celebration.
with me in the background – Feb. 2001

WRAMC Compound 2001

PART III

CHAPTER 9

MY MILITARY LIFE BEGINS

Finally! A new chapter, in which I could pursue my dream and make a difference. As a member of the military, I felt like someone who would give for her country—President Kennedy's inauguration speech from so long ago was still a standard I wanted to live up to. And at the same time, I was declaring my own independence and taking charge of my future, just as my father had hoped I would do when we arrived from Saudi Arabia.

My nerves were shot after dealing with the trauma, abuse, and stress of my so-called "marriage," and my attempts to be accepted had failed throughout my life thus far. This new path could get me there, but my worries started to build. What if it were more of the same? At the time, divorce in the military was frowned upon, and your commanding officer had the full backing of the US government to scream at you. Every day as I approached mustering in, I was a little more apprehensive. I finally decided to move forward and jump into my next phase.

It took several weeks for my application to be processed along with the entrance physical and background check for my security clearance. Once everything was completed and approved, I took my oath of office with Sarah and Lawrie proudly standing in as my witnesses as I accepted a direct commission as a captain.

I received orders to report for basic training at Fort Sam Houston (known informally as Fort Sam) in San Antonio, Texas, then on to Washington, DC for my first assignment.

Leaving Kokomo was bittersweet. The bitter part was that I had a few close friends and coworkers I would leave behind, and of course, I would dearly miss Sarah and Lawrie. But how sweet to now have an ex-husband—and I couldn't wait to be as far away from him as I possibly could. Before I left, I gave Nadir a quit-claim deed in exchange for half the equity of the house.

The most difficult part, undoubtedly, was that I would have to be separated from Hannah and Amal while I was in San Antonio. Mutti and Vati were still living in Petersburg, and I drove the girls there so they could stay with their grandparents while I was in basic training. I also enrolled them in preschool because I didn't want them staying home all day without social interaction with other children. Most of all, I didn't want to burden my parents with caring for two active toddlers all day.

My father was in hemodialysis treatments three times a week. Despite his serious medical problem, he was elated to have his granddaughters with him for a few weeks. It was hard to tell how my mother felt about it—she was never one to show her emotions. I called the girls every evening at bedtime and reassured them that Mommy would soon be back with them.

BASIC TRAINING

Before I could be an Army nurse, I had to learn to be a soldier and an officer. That's what basic training is designed to do. Our six-week officer training program for the Army Medical Department (AMEDD) was conducted at the Academy of Health Sciences at

Fort Sam. There were about 100 officers in my class; it was a good mix of doctors, nurses, dentists, veterinarians, and physical therapists.

On our first day, we received a general introduction to Army lifestyle and an overview of how our training would proceed. The first thing I learned was the AMEDD's motto: "To Conserve the Fighting Strength." I adapted quickly to Army culture: Learning about the history of military medicine, how to march, how and when to salute, and how to wear the various uniforms, including minute details on where to place rank, pins, and patches down to the fraction of an inch felt natural to me. We had classroom instruction and practical exercises, followed by written exams.

Once classes were over for the day, my time was my own. I had been so isolated during my marriage but now I enjoyed getting to know my fellow officers and making new friends. We went out for dinner on San Antonio's famous Riverwalk. We went to nightclubs to hear music. I still loved to dance and took the opportunity to learn Texas line dancing. I felt free again, much as I did when I was at SFSU.

Being in the Army is a tough way to experience a physical rebirth in the sense of getting back into shape. The military had demanding fitness standards. At 115 pounds, I didn't have a weight problem, but the Army took fitness seriously—being thin and being fit are two very different things. During my six weeks in basic, I learned to appreciate the importance of exercise, not simply to meet the fitness standard and pass the tests but as a habit to maintain throughout my career. My time in San Antonio was absolutely a rebirth of my spirit and my independence as well.

WHAT RELIGION AM I?

There was an avalanche of paperwork to complete: A will, power of attorney, military ID card, emergency data form, family care plan, etc. These were part of my Soldier Readiness Plan (SRP), and it was my responsibility to keep it current. Then there were the dog tags. The two metal tags had duplicate ID information, including name, rank, social security number, and blood type. They were to be worn at all times. We each had two tags so that if there was a casualty in the field, one could be taken for notification purposes while the other would be left on the body.

Dog tags also indicated religious preference, and for me, this was a ticking time bomb. My official Army records indicated that I had been born in Egypt and that I was a naturalized US citizen. My background check and security clearance did as well. There was nothing in my file or official record that indicated my religion—yet.

The dog tags would be the first. I was a Muslim, but I didn't want that on my tags. Ever since the OPEC oil embargo and the Iranian revolution in the 1970s followed by the hostage crisis of 1980, the words "Arab," "Islam," and "Muslim" had become synonymous with "nefarious," "harmful," and "destructive" in most Americans' minds. My day-to-day concern was that within the Army, my faith would single me out for discrimination, and I'd already had more than enough of that growing up. In a broader sense, I was also worried about my personal safety, a fear made more intense by the fact that I was the single parent of two young children. If we ever came into conflict with an Islamic nation or Islamic insurgent group, it would be potentially dangerous, even deadly, for me to be identified as both a Muslim and a member of the US Armed Forces. I thought about what might happen to me if I were captured, and the unnecessary risk wasn't worth it.

I called my father for advice. "I understand your desire to get around this, *ya habibti*," he began. "It's important to be treated fairly and equally. Tell them you don't belong to any particular religion but that you believe in one God and consider yourself to be a spiritual person."

The next day I tried to explain to the processing sergeant what my father had said. "Can't do it," he grumbled, shaking his head. "Not enough room. It's either Protestant, Catholic, or Jewish. Which is it, Captain Johnson?" Seeing my hesitation, he added, "If you don't want any of those choices, I can put NRP instead."

"What's NRP?" I asked, perplexed at the acronym.

"It means 'No Religious Preference,'" the sergeant replied.

"Okay, that sounds good. NRP it is!" Even though I was relieved that this matter had been resolved, I was left with an uneasy feeling. To blend in and have a fair chance at becoming successful and equal, I had to hide my heritage once again.

* * * * *

Soon enough, I experienced the rigors of Field Training Exercises (FTX), which included everything from battlefield simulations to survival skills. The exercise was conducted at Camp Bullis, roughly 25 miles southwest of San Antonio, and we were driven to the camp in open military trucks.

Once we arrived, we were divided into squads and assigned to shared tents. I made friends with another captain named Vien, who was also an OB nurse. Originally from Vietnam, she was a recent widow with two young sons who were a little older than Hannah and Amal. It would be a week of roughing it—we lived in our fatigues. Improvised field showers were limited to a few minutes every other day, and we ate our meals outdoors.

We received practical skills training in how to transfer and carry patients on a litter. We also had two half-day sessions at the firing range where we learned marksmanship and weapons safety. After shooting an assigned set of magazines, we learned how to break down, clean, and reassemble our weapons. In addition, each of us was given individual and group lessons in map and compass reading and how to navigate obstacle courses. During a night training exercise, our squad piled into a deuce and a half (an army truck), and we were taken to a remote area of the camp. We were each issued a compass, a map, and a flashlight. Our assignment was to find our home base from there as a group, only using these three tools. Somehow, Vien and I got separated from the rest of our squad and became hopelessly lost. A rescue team was sent out and found us several hours later.

* * * * *

ANOTHER ASSASSINATED LEADER

I was still in basic training when I heard that Egyptian president Anwar Sadat had been assassinated. October 6, 1981was a tragic day for Sadat's family and for Egypt and changed the balance of world peace. It was also a day of great sadness for my father, Sadat's friend from so long ago. I called my parents immediately after hearing the news. Vati was shaken and tearful as we spoke. He didn't say much, except to express his love and gratitude for this man. It was the eight-year anniversary of the start of the Yom Kippur war.

Losing Sadat tore at Vati's heart—the last time they'd seen each other was their reunion visit eight years before. I, too, was disappointed and saddened because I'd hoped that sometime during my military career, I'd have an opportunity to meet with this great leader of modern Egypt and my father's good friend.

I wanted to share my sadness with military colleagues. I wanted to let them know that there are people in the Middle East who are exceptional individuals and shouldn't be painted with a broad brush, but I decided it was best to keep it to myself. I didn't know how it would be perceived, and I couldn't risk being an outcast once again.

CHAPTER 10

YOU'RE *REALLY* IN THE ARMY NOW

The six weeks of basic training went by quickly, but I couldn't wait to see my family again. Graduation took place on October 14, and I returned to Virginia the next day to be reunited with my daughters and my parents.

Nadir saw my time in basic training as an opportunity to try to weasel out of his financial obligations to his children, the first of many such attempts. I'd been in San Antonio less than two weeks when my attorney in Kokomo notified me that Nadir had filed a court petition to terminate child support.

Nadir's income wasn't the issue. He earned a comfortable, upper middle-class salary, but as far as he was concerned, his income was his and his alone. The way he saw it, the girls and I were not entitled to any financial support whatsoever. He wanted me, along with *my* children, to live in poverty, and he said so outright. What kind of vile human being would wish that for his children and their mother? One who'd learned it at his father's knee. Nadir actually told me that he hoped I would end up "in the streets as a beggar like those whores and their bastard children who used to come to my father to beg for food and money."

My attorney told me he'd never seen a case like this and that Nadir's own lawyer was frustrated by his client's blatant refusal to pay child support. Regardless of how many times Nadir's attorney tried to explain to him that he had to pay, he continued to try any angle he could to avoid it. The bottom line was that despite being a US citizen, he didn't believe US law should apply to him. In his own mind, he was above it all.

After a week of leave, I reported to my new assignment at Walter Reed Army Medical Center (WRAMC) in Washington, DC, a little over two hours from my parents' house. I left the girls with them until I could get settled in.

Because people in the military move around frequently, the act of settling in has been systematized by the Army. The procedure, called in-processing, is completed within a few days as the soldier stops at each predetermined station for information and instructions regarding housing, finance, and personal matters such as travel expenses, vehicle registration, and parking. When it's time to leave a post, the procedure is reversed and is known as out-processing.

Securing permanent housing in this high-cost area was a problem. A single parent with a limited budget looking at mortgage interest rates at 15% was going to have a hard time finding an affordable place to live in the DC area. For my daughters' sake, I had to be fastidious about neighborhoods and schools; I preferred a smaller, modest home in a safe neighborhood to a larger home in a less desirable area. I was able to find a two-bedroom, one-bath duplex in Wheaton, Maryland, only a few miles from WRAMC, and I used the settlement money from my divorce as a down payment.

As soon as I brought the girls to the house, they ran upstairs and found their room. I'd already done my best to make it theirs before they ever saw it—I furnished and decorated it with their favorite colors, toys, and characters like Strawberry Shortcake. They were happy, which meant I was happy. Although my new home was small, it was cozy and full of love and peace. At last, I had peace in my home and tranquility in my mind. And for the first time in my life, I felt like I didn't have to compare myself to anyone in order to feel equal to my peers. In the Army, rank structure and number of years served determined one's salary; not gender, religion, or ethnic background.

Phyllis and Charlie Hoffman were a warm and friendly elderly couple who lived in the other half of the duplex. Not surprisingly, they found Hannah and Amal precious and adorable—at ages two and four, of course they were.

* * * * *

When I arrived at WRAMC in October 1981, the new hospital was less than five years old. This gargantuan building was the flagship of the Army medical service with five inpatient floors and two levels dedicated to outpatient services, over a million square feet of floor space, and state-of-the-art equipment. The main hospital entrance resembled a huge shopping mall with a two-story foyer and mezzanine. It was as busy as a mall, too, with people constantly coming and going. The long corridors reminded me of airport concourses.

My first assignment was on Ward 67, a gynecological unit primarily for oncology patients with rare, unusual, or terminal diseases who were active duty, dependents, retirees, and patients from foreign allied forces from all over the world. Vien was posted there as well.

We were busy with challenging cases, but this was the kind of work I'd envisioned doing when I became a nurse. I loved my job, but the scheduling was difficult and at times impossible. The general policy of the Department of Nursing at WRAMC was to rotate shifts. Because of the girls, I chose day and night shifts. That way I could have evenings free to spend with them. Soon, however, we were hit with a staff shortage, which meant I had to accept some evening shifts as well. And as with most staff nursing jobs anywhere, we also had to work alternate weekends and often on holidays.

This threw my childcare arrangements into a tailspin. The Army requires us to have a family care plan, but my constantly changing schedule made it impossible to maintain the one I'd set up. There weren't many reliable caregivers who wanted to deal with rotating shifts, fewer still who were willing to work on weekends and holidays. Daycare centers weren't an option since they were geared to parents who worked normal business hours—the "day" part of daycare.

There were times when I simply couldn't find anyone to be with my daughters. There were also times, especially if I was working the night shift, when the sitter I'd hired flaked out on me and didn't show up. When it came time for me to leave for work and she hadn't arrived, I awakened the girls from their sleep and took them with me. What else was I supposed to do? I certainly didn't want to be late for work, and calling in to say I couldn't report for duty wasn't an option—this was, after all, the Army. On the nights when I arrived at WRAMC with the girls, I made up a little bed for them in the nurses' station lounge.

This made my head nurse, a major, most unhappy with me. "Captain Johnson! It's your responsibility to have an effective family care plan and to have reliable childcare arrangements made. Do you understand?" she'd ask.

"Yes, ma'am," I replied. I was annoyed at her lack of empathy but knew better than to let that show. "I've tried," I continued.

"But what should I do if my babysitter doesn't show up? I've had several different babysitters who've failed to arrive—they don't even call ahead of time to tell me. I can't leave my daughters home alone."

"That's *not* the Army's problem!" she snapped. "If the Army wanted you to have children, they'd have issued them to you."

I soon learned this was an old Army cliché, but like most clichés, it was rooted in a kernel of truth. As far as my head nurse was concerned, everything had to be by the book. She reminded me of Major Margaret "Hot Lips" Houlihan from the TV show, *M*A*S*H*, except that there was nothing funny about it. Each time I brought my daughters to work, she wrote me up.

My first Christmas as a single parent was not only memorable but emotionally significant. Finally, I felt free—free to uphold our family traditions, free to decorate our home and our Christmas tree without judgment, opinion, or restriction, free to visit with my parents, free from Nadir's relentless criticisms. My parents spent a few days with us during the holidays, and I arranged for a couple of dialysis sessions for my father at a nearby medical clinic to make sure he was able to enjoy the visit. As we counted down the days to Christmas, Hannah and Amal could barely contain themselves. They were excited about decorating the tree, helping me bake cookies, and most certainly about the coming of Santa Claus.

I was content with my new life and happy to be free of Nadir but he did call me several times. During one of his calls, he pleaded with me to reconcile "for the sake of the children." However delusional his thinking was, I was still sad for Hannah and Amal. When Nadir divorced me, he pretty much divorced them as well. He'd never been much of a father to his daughters, but now that we were no longer married, he stopped being a father at all. He never called to speak to them. He never once sent a card, letter, or gift to either of them. As upset as that made me, a reconciliation wasn't going to happen—nor was it even possible, seeing as he'd already remarried.

Nadir didn't tell me though. I had stayed in touch with Sarah and Lawrie, my former next-door neighbors in Kokomo. Sarah informed me that Nadir had traveled to Egypt and come back with a new bride, Miriam. Sarah had seen her in passing a few times and said that she seemed quiet, sweet, and friendly. My guess was that this was the *anessa* that Nadir's parents had picked out for him while he was still married to me.

When I told Nadir I was aware that he had remarried, he reverted to his usual pattern of denials, excuses, and lies. He announced that his new marriage was a mistake and lamented that he wished we could be together. I was disgusted by his deceitfulness and suspected that his calls were part of his never-ending campaign to get out of paying child support.

The prospect of the first court-ordered summer visitation filled me with fear and trepidation. Nadir had often threatened to take the girls out of the country and then vanish. Even though I'd kept their social security numbers, I worried—this monthlong summer visitation was a perfect opportunity to make good on his evil promise. I dreaded their departure, but I was well aware that if I displayed any kind of discomfort or anxiety, they'd sense it.

In June 1982, Nadir was due to arrive at the door to pick up Hannah and Amal. Four weeks later, I would return to Kokomo to retrieve them and bring them back home.

I tried to prepare them ahead of time, since they hadn't seen or spoken to their father since we left Kokomo.

"I don't remember what he looks like," Amal admitted on the morning they were to leave. Their suitcases, sitting on the floor by the doorway, were packed with all the clothes and toys they'd need for the next four weeks.

"You will when you see him," I assured her. "It'll all come back to you."

"Do we have to go, Mommy?" Hannah asked.

"Yes, darling, I have to allow you to go. Besides, don't you want to know your Papa better too?" I answered.

I tried to sound as sunny as possible without letting on that my heart was breaking inside.

It didn't matter. When Nadir rang the bell and I opened the door, the girls fled from him and began to cry. Nadir didn't look any happier about this arrangement than they did. He stood at the door like a statue; he did nothing to alleviate their fears. He also did nothing to help get them into his car. I had to physically pick up each girl, and they both fought me furiously, kicking and shrieking in abject terror as I buckled them into their car seats.

It wasn't hard to understand how they felt. Their mother was handing them over to a man who was pretty much a perfect stranger. Their wailing was loud enough to attract the attention of our neighbors, who gathered to stare at the spectacle. I felt like my heart was ripping out of my chest because there was nothing I could do to console them.

True to form, Nadir lit up a cigarette and watched, detached and impassive. As soon as I had buckled the girls into the car, he got behind the wheel. Without saying a word, he pulled away from the curb. I could still hear my daughters crying as the car receded into the distance.

I immediately called Sarah in Kokomo and explained what had gone on and how frightened I was.

Sarah promised that she and Lawrie would be my eyes and ears while Hannah and Amal stayed next door. She also gave me her word that she'd talk to the new wife regularly to assess the situation.

Even after I'd talked to Sarah, dread washed over me in waves. I was afraid that I'd seen my daughters for the last time and that I had aided and abetted their kidnapping. What had I done?

* * * * *

HEMODIALYSIS

Meanwhile, my father's renal dialysis was dominating my parents' schedule, taking up to six hours a day, three days a week. He was also beginning to have chest pains and other cardiac symptoms. Vati's need for extensive treatment was serious enough that his doctors recommended to my parents that they move closer to the teams of specialists essential to his care. Even after the move, my father continued to drive the half-hour to work at Fort Lee, taking medical leave for his dialysis days. Luckily, his job and his supervisors were flexible enough to allow him to work part time at his own pace. I was most appreciative of their empathetic understanding. Vati didn't just love his work—he needed it to give him a sense of purpose.

In Richmond, my father had a new team of physicians, led by a cardiologist and a nephrologist. Within weeks, they had arranged for my mother to receive specialized training in how to give hemodialysis at home, which was far more comfortable and less time-consuming than driving to a center. Once she initiated the dialysis, she could keep my father company while doing her household chores and cooking. It made life better for both of them.

* * * * *

I made it a point to call my daughters every day. Each time I called, we counted down the days, and this helped alleviate my own fears. I also spoke with Nadir's new wife, Miriam, several times. She sounded soft-spoken and sincere, reassuring me she would watch over my daughters.

When the month was up, I drove to Kokomo to bring the girls home again. When I rang the doorbell, I heard them scampering towards the door, calling out, "Mommy! Mommy! It's Mommy!" A few seconds later, the door opened and the girls jetted out to me. They jumped up and down, delighted to see me, and I was just as excited to see them. To hug them, to kiss them, and to hold them in my arms was pure joy. Pure love. An indescribable love.

A few minutes after the joyous reunion, I heard the storm door open again. It was Miriam. She placed the girls' suitcases and bags of toys on the step and smiled.

"Nice to meet you," I said as I reached out my hand to shake hers. That, apparently, was too much for her. I sensed her hesitation and pulled my hand back. "Thank you for being so good with my daughters," I added. "And for keeping me up to date about them during our telephone conversations."

"It was nice to have them," she replied. "They are very cute."

I asked them how the visit was and if they got to spend some fun time with their father.

"He didn't talk to us much," Hannah announced.

"Yeah, and he was hardly ever home," Amal added.

My daughters said they had enjoyed their time with Miriam, which took the sting off.

As Miriam was getting ready to say something, I heard Nadir's voice in the background. He never appeared, just yelled out to Miriam, ordering her to get away from the door and shut it. She jumped at his voice and did as she was told. I sensed her fear and slowly backed away from the doorway.

It didn't matter that I had escaped from my horrible situation, I flashed back to my own experience of being screamed at and flinching. As Miriam looked at me and shut the door, I couldn't help but feel sick to my stomach. I prayed that Miriam would find her way to freedom one day.

* * * * *

As the weeks went by, I struggled with rotating shifts and unreliable babysitters, which made for a stressful routine. Childcare problems were a constant issue. I felt so alone as a single parent, and even worse, I felt like no one cared—certainly not the Army. There seemed to be no way to reconcile being a good parent with having an Army career. As much as I loved my work, I often broke down and cried when I got home. Phyllis and Charlie were my last resort; they kept the girls at their home if I had last-minute no-shows or no other options.

The Hoffmans were helpful in other ways as well. When Phyllis made soup or a casserole, she often made enough for us to eat. And if she saw a cute little toy she thought the girls might like, she bought it for them. Charlie took pride in building a slide and swing set for the girls in the backyard we shared, and he always had the biggest smile on his face as he watched the girls enjoying it. Sometimes when he mowed his lawn, he went ahead and mowed my half too. In the winter, he shoveled the snow on my walkway.

Charlie even made sure I had a place to park. We didn't have a driveway or garage, and as in most DC suburbs, street parking was hard to come by. As a general rule, the first residents who got home in the evenings got the best parking spaces. Late arrivals often ended up parking many blocks from home, but the Hoffmans ran their errands early in the day and were usually home by early afternoon. When they arrived, they intentionally parked in a way that took up two parking spaces, making it impossible for anyone else to park in front or behind them. When they knew

I was due home, one of them sat by the window and watched for my car. As I pulled up, Charlie moved his car up a few feet, enough to make a space for me. I was truly grateful to have these angels in my life. They cherished the girls, and I cherished the Hoffmans. I felt so blessed.

Vien eventually helped me solve my childcare problem. She told me that she had several family members who lived nearby, most of whom had recently immigrated from Vietnam. She said the women stayed home all day with their small children and that they'd be willing to look after Hannah and Amal while I was at work.

After meeting Vien's family, I accepted their offer. It was a huge weight off my shoulders, and from then on, they provided the dependable childcare I needed to help me take care of my girls and focus on my job. They were honest, kind, and reliable but most importantly, they genuinely loved my daughters. They treated us as though we were a part of their family and were very flexible, even with my crazy schedule—days, evenings, nights, weekends, and holidays. I felt much more secure and confident that I could continue serving in the Army as a single parent, although the Army never did make it easy.

Now with daycare not being such a worry, a big decision in my life was about to help move my goal towards equality and advancement in the right direction. Vien and I participated in the annual FTX, which was a regular component of being on active duty. It lasted several days.

While there, Vien told me about a new program the Army offered to train nurses to become nurse practitioners (NP). The NP concept was an advancement that wasn't only new to the Army but also relatively new to nursing itself. In the civilian sector, NP programs were often tied to graduate programs at universities and usually 18 months long. Successful completion resulted in a master's degree. The Army's program was condensed into a six-month curriculum with a certificate of completion rather than a master's degree; it was offered twice a year with specialties in obstetrics and gynecology (OB/GYN), pediatrics, adult and family health. Vien had already been accepted and she left for Fort Bragg, North Carolina in January 1983. Fortunately for me, her family stayed near Walter Reed and they were happy to continue helping me take care of my children.

I went to the chief of the Nursing Education Department at WRAMC and officially applied. I was accepted into the next class after Vien's class, which was scheduled to begin in July 1983. The bad news was that there was no way to complete this rigid program and take care of two young children.

When I telephoned my parents to tell them the exciting news, my father immediately offered to take care of my daughters while I was at Fort Bragg.

"That way you can devote your full time to your studies," Vati told me.

As soon as I received my acceptance into the NP program and my orders, I tried to prepare the girls for the transition.

"We have to move because Mommy has to attend an Army course for six months in another state called North Carolina," I explained to them as I saw the confusion on their little faces. Although they understood we were going to move again, I realized they were not quite old enough to grasp the concept of how long six months was. "That means from the time I start the school in July until Christmas," I explained. "We have to move out of this house first, and you two get to stay with Oma and Opa while Mommy is at the school!"

I tried to make the girls and myself feel better by repeatedly telling them how fast six months would pass. The girls don't even remember our separation but I still remember it to this day.

CHAPTER 11

BACK TO SCHOOL IN THE DEEP SOUTH

Bustling with over 50,000 active-duty personnel, Fort Bragg is home to several famous Army units, most notably Special Operations Command and the 82nd Airborne Division. It is also the home of Womack Army Medical Center, which was known as Womack Army Community Hospital in 1983.

Despite the elite groups on the base, the civilian area nearby was rundown. The street leading up to the main gate was lined with squalid buildings and seedy establishments—pawn shops, strip clubs, dive bars, and cheap motels. Women hung out in front of these businesses dressed in tawdry clothing. Their profession was obvious. An assortment of pathetic and disreputable characters careened unsteadily past them. Many clutched a brown paper bag in one hand, swigging from bottles, the bags only partly concealed. I missed my daughters already, but I was happy I didn't have to explain this to them.

Once I reported to Womack Hospital, I met the three other women in my class. Like me, they were young captains. We were all eager to learn and eager to take our places among the Army's first NPs. Our two instructors, a major and a captain, were equally enthusiastic and determined to help us excel. They were exceptionally kind and patient with all of us.

The program was intense. We had to master in six months the same information that most university graduate programs taught over 18 months. The mornings started early with an hour of mandatory PT before the day's instruction began. Days were spent either in class or clinical practice. Evenings were spent studying and completing assigned papers. By the time I returned each night from the library, I was exhausted. I climbed into bed and fell asleep quickly—another long day would start before dawn.

Despite the rigorous schedule, I made a point of making the three-hour drive to Richmond every other weekend to see my daughters. I missed the girls so much and longed for their tender hugs and kisses. I missed looking into their beautiful, loving eyes and hearing their little voices say, "I love you, Mommy." I missed my parents too. When I described the difficulty of the courses, my father, as always, continued to support me. He reminded me to stay focused on my goal. Each visit enabled me to return to Fort Bragg charged with new resolve.

At the beginning of the program, we were assigned a research project to be completed by the end of the term. The subject I chose was "Cultural Aspects of Arab Women in the US Healthcare System." The topic was not only important to military healthcare providers, it was also close to my heart. At the time, there were increasing numbers of Arab exchange officers, soldiers, and their families, who were stationed with US forces, both here and overseas. I knew firsthand how challenging it was to make yourself understood when you're plunged into a strange culture. It's scary enough when you're healthy—if you're unwell, it can be truly frightening.

My paper presented new and useful information. It was well received by my instructors and colleagues. And their expressions as I presented indicated that they were as stunned as I had been to learn of the practice of "female circumcision" by some Arab and African cultures.

By the time graduation arrived, I had already received orders for Fort McClellan, Alabama and I was delighted. In my new duty station, I would function in the role of OB/GYN (now known as women's health care) NP, which meant clinic days and clinic hours of Monday through Friday, 7:30 a.m. to 4:30 p.m. It was exactly what I had hoped for: a regular schedule and more time with my girls.

* * * * *

Fort McClellan was one of the oldest military installations in the country. Located in northeastern Alabama near the city of Anniston, it was training headquarters for military police and for the Chemical Corps. It was also the home of the Women's Army Corps. Fort McClellan closed in 1999 as part of the Army Base Closure and Realignment Committee (BRAC) legislation.

I purchased a four-bedroom ranch from a retiring Army chaplain whose hobby was woodworking. He had made numerous improvements to the house. It was well maintained and perfect for me and my girls. Hannah and Amal were excited to see their rooms and backyard. I was excited, too, especially because excellent before- and after-school programs were readily available. This was a huge relief; my days of dealing with unreliable sitters were over.

I loved my new position in the Noble Army Community Hospital clinic. My boss was a young, southern-raised OB/GYN physician with a friendly disposition and a great sense of humor.

I was worried about moving to Anniston as it had a history of racial tension. In the early days of the civil rights movement, a bus carrying Freedom Riders was firebombed in Anniston; the passengers were beaten with chains and crowbars as they tried to escape the burning bus.

Segregationist mob violence had continued for the next several years, but that shameful part of the city's history was nowhere in evidence while I was stationed there. I felt welcomed in Anniston, not only by my colleagues and coworkers but also by my neighbors, the local merchants, and everyone at the school Hannah and Amal attended. The neighbors and mothers of young children greeted and accepted us readily, as if we'd lived there forever. They invited us to join them for picnics, lunches, and dinners on weekends. Although I hadn't known quite what to expect when I arrived, everyone made me feel part of this community. Anniston was unquestionably rooted in the tradition of hospitality of the Deep South.

Still, I wondered if I should let others know that we were Muslim. I didn't like the idea of deception but I eventually chose not to say. My daughters' safety was at risk. I didn't even talk to Hannah and Amal about Islam, lest they brought it up at school or with one of their friends. Their last name at the time was still Marwan, and when people asked about the origin of the name or where I was born, I simply said Egypt. I didn't elaborate, and since Egypt had large Christian and Jewish populations, I let people draw their own conclusions.

I did talk to Hannah and Amal about my strong belief in a higher being, a higher "Oneness" that created us and everything else in the universe. I answered their questions about God as straightforwardly as I could. Before meals we recited together "God is great, God is good, thank you God, for our food." I taught them simple prayers and reassured them that they were always loved and protected by God. I also drew on some of the Sufi parables my father had taught me, stories that showed how each of us is unique in our individual gifts and talents and has something special to offer the world. In essence, I talked to my girls about spirituality rather than about any particular religion.

Life in Anniston was peaceful and calm. Our daily routine as a family of three went on with relative ease.

My work was fulfilling and rewarding—there was a strong spirit of camaraderie at the clinic. I also had a lot more time to spend with my daughters, and I soon learned that one of the favorite pastimes in the South was entering little girls into beauty pageants. Friends, neighbors, and mothers of children who went to school with my daughters tried to persuade me to enter Hannah and Amal into some of the local pageants, but I declined. I didn't explain my refusal of these well-intentioned offers but to me it was a matter of principle. I felt that active participation in the pageant system gave young girls the wrong message. I wanted my daughters to be educated, to excel, and to succeed on the merits of their character and their critical thinking skills, not on how cute they were. This was similar to my father's ambition for me—that I should have the same opportunity for education as my brothers so that I could become an independent, self-sufficient adult.

Nevertheless, living in the South was having an effect on the girls, in particular on their speech patterns. One evening I was taking advantage of the last few minutes of daylight to pull weeds out of a flowerbed. The girls were helping. While kneeling on the ground, I felt Amal's arms wrap around my neck to give me a hug and a tender, sweet kiss on my cheek.

"Mommy, is the sun fixin' to go down?" she asked in a sweet drawl that sounded like an Anniston native. My heart melted.

"Yes, sweetheart, the sun is fixin' to go down," I answered, hugging her close to me. Feeling the vibration of undeniable, unconditional love between me and my girls was bliss. I was so grateful for this moment and for my time with them here in Anniston.

The girls were happy in their school and with their new friends. I had time to help them with their homework. I planned activities for the weekends like going to the park, the zoo, or swimming at the officers' club as a family, just the three of us.

ANOTHER SUMMER VISIT WITH NADIR

All too soon, however, it was time for the girls' annual trip to Indiana. The girls resisted—although they'd been there twice before, they didn't want to go. I didn't want them to go either. Despite my apprehensiveness, I knew I had to comply with the directive from the court. Nadir also stuck to his old familiar pattern—all year long, he evinced no interest whatsoever in his daughters and had no contact with them. He was also skipping some of his child support payments.

By the time the girls went for their fourth summer visit, there seemed to be a repeat of the old familiar patterns with new twists. Nadir now repeatedly fell behind on child support payments. Whenever that happened, I had to get my attorney to write a letter informing him that he was in arrears, and *I* had to pay the lawyer for every letter he wrote. With each summer visitation, there was also a bit of news. It was always the same news—a new baby. Miriam bore Nadir three children in quick succession—all girls. The male chauvinist who so desperately wanted a son had now sired five daughters. To me, this was a bit of divine cosmic comeuppance. Karma, if you will. Still, for Miriam's sake, and for the sake of her daughters, I hoped that Nadir was calmer and a better father this time around. On second thought, fat chance, I quickly realized.

I remembered all too well how angry Nadir became each time he learned his newborn child was female and how eager he was to let me know that this was entirely my fault. Given that Nadir had evolved little, if at all, in the time we were married, it seemed highly unlikely that his attitude toward girls and women would have suddenly improved.

While my daughters were in Kokomo, I called Miriam on my lunch hour to check on them. Her English was still tentative, but mixed with Arabic, we managed to communicate fine. Miriam always went out of her way to reassure me that Hannah and Amal were fine. Then she put them on the phone, one at a time, so I could speak to them. Each girl talked happily about playing with her half-sisters. I appreciated everything Miriam was doing for them, and I let her know that.

* * * * *

While I was stationed at Fort McClellan, I began dating, ever so tentatively. But it never worked out, even when it seemed promising at the outset. One particularly miserable experience occurred with Michael, whom I dated several times until he casually let it slip that he thought Hannah "wasn't Aryan enough."

My eyes flashed—"Aryan" was a term out of Hitler's Germany. "What do you mean by not Aryan enough?" I asked incredulously. "Not Aryan enough for what or for whom?"

Michael was taken aback by the vehemence of my response. He became defensive, fumbling for words as he tried to placate me. "I mean, she's so much *darker* than her sister," he began.

"What?" I snapped.

"And, well, darker than we are," he continued.

"She's my daughter, for God's sake!" I shot back. "What do you propose that I do with her, dip her in bleach?"

As the old proverb goes, when you're in a hole, stop digging. Could it be that Michael really had no idea that his explanation only made it worse? In that moment, our relationship blew up, at least my side of it did. If this man truly believed that I had a daughter who wasn't "Aryan enough," there was no chance of a relationship, much less another date. I looked at him with aversion and disgust, and then I left.

Trying to find the bright side, as my father had taught me to do, I thanked God that this man had revealed himself as a bigot before our relationship got any further than it did.

Although I had been treated well in Anniston, it wasn't uncommon to hear the "N" word used by some white locals. It disgusted me and whenever I had the opportunity, I let people know how offensive this word was to me. That epithet had been flung at me and my brothers both in St. Louis and in Inglewood. Although it had happened years ago, it was still all too easy for me to summon up the pain and shame I felt at the time.

Then there was my father. When he learned about a date that went past 9:00 p.m., I would be admonished for not being lady-like and following our cultural norms. In spite of his progressive view on women's education, he couldn't shake the ultraconservative cultural and social values of the past. Since I was 33 by now, I stood my ground. Mutti had no comments at all.

* * * * *

At Christmastime 1984, my parents came to Anniston to spend the holidays with us. Other than my father's regular dialysis treatments, it was truly a festive time of family togetherness. All the students at school made ornaments as presents for their parents. I baked cookies for Hannah and Amal's classroom Christmas parties and also baked plenty for us to enjoy at home. We all decorated the Christmas tree together. Hannah and Amal proudly hung the special decorations they had made in school. Watching how happy my daughters and parents were gave me so much joy. This was a very good time in my life.

Fort McClellan was one of my favorite assignments in my Army career. That said, there were still a few bumps along the way. One of them came in the form of a "dining in," or regimental mess, which was a longstanding military tradition that we inherited from the British.

It started back when redcoats and muskets were still in fashion, if not before. The purpose of the dinner was to enhance unit cohesion, camaraderie, and esprit de corps. It was a major event on the Fort McClellan social calendar that included officers and noncoms from every unit on post. Strictly speaking, I was not "required" to go. Attendance was, however, "highly recommended," which we all knew was code for "mandatory." Those who skipped out risked being labeled "not a team player," which was a huge black mark when you came up for promotion. I wasn't looking forward to attending an "advisable" formal dinner, but in the interest of preserving my chances of becoming a career officer, I put on my dress blues and showed up.

The evening followed time-honored tradition. There were many toasts to which everyone responded, "hear, hear!" followed by a sip of the port wine that had been pre-poured for us. Gradually, the toasts got more absurd and humorous—eventually, any oration was little more than an excuse to take a drink. Those who didn't drink alcohol toasted with water instead, but for those who did, the sips became gulps and spirits such as gin or vodka replaced the port wine.

Not surprisingly, numerous officers proceeded to get very, very inebriated. The evening then became terribly uncomfortable for me and the few other women present. As the event progressed,

I found myself surrounded by several male officers who were so sloshed they thought it was okay to put their hands all over me, kissing me, and making sexual gestures and lewd remarks.

I fought off the various hands stroking, caressing, and embracing me. As I looked around for someone to rescue me, the assaults only worsened and heightened in intensity. The other women, I saw, weren't faring any better.

The repulsive realization that I had paid to be groped and propositioned by drunks who outranked me was my signal to leave. The rest of the women followed suit.

McClellan's senior officers attended these events but they didn't intervene. No one in authority told these lecherous sots that their behavior was unbecoming or that it bordered on sexual assault. As disgusting as these episodes were, we female officers didn't dare report the offenders. We were cowed into silence for the same reason we kept going to these testosterone-fueled boys' club binges—so that we would be seen as "team players" when we were evaluated for advancement. There is a code of silence around this unacceptable behavior, which in part is why it has persisted for so long.

In February 1985, Vati's condition began to decline. He started having more frequent episodes of chest pain, severe enough to wake him from his sleep. After he was diagnosed with congestive heart failure, he became depressed. Realizing that his entire life now revolved around dealing with his medical conditions— heart problems on top of kidney disease—he became progressively weaker and less engaged in day-to-day activities. Although she never complained to me about it, my mother was also extremely stressed by her responsibilities as Vati's full-time caregiver.

I felt sad for them, and the fact that they were in Richmond alone without any of their children nearby for support made it worse. All four of my brothers were in California. I tried to take leave as often as I could but living in Anniston, over 600 miles away, made it difficult. It was a long day's drive to get there and another day to drive back. I was burning through my accrued leave time, and I had to save a few days to get the girls to and from Kokomo for court-ordered visitation.

I mentioned my predicament to a colleague over lunch. "I know someone who recently faced a similar family situation," he said. "He requested and received a compassionate reassignment. You might want to check into that."

"But I've only been assigned to Fort McClellan for a little over a year," I replied. It seemed highly unlikely that my request would be approved.

"You should at least look into it. Otherwise, you'll never know."

I met with my immediate supervisors and filled out the forms I needed to complete. I asked for a position as an NP because I didn't want to go back to a staff nurse position with rotating shifts and weekend duty and the childcare nightmare that schedule created. I requested assignment to Fort Belvoir, Virginia, not far from Richmond. Walter Reed in DC and Fort Meade in Maryland were my second and third choices.

My request was approved, and I was ordered to report to Fort Meade by the end of July 1985.

PROMOTION TO MAJOR

Before leaving Anniston, I learned that I'd been selected for promotion to major. I was exhilarated and extremely proud, knowing that my hard work and dedication had been recognized and rewarded. Throughout my time at Fort McClellan, I had done as much as I could to make sure my superiors knew I wanted to be a career officer. I took continuing education and officer advanced training courses by correspondence. These courses matter once you're up for promotion because they indicated a desire to continue advancing and a willingness to take on more responsibility. I'd gone through the head nurse training program at Fort Sam for the same reason.

The actual promotion ceremony is steeped in tradition and highly personal at the same time. In the Army Nurse Corps, it is customary to have your new rank pinned on by two people, one for each shoulder. One is to be a higher-ranking officer and I chose my hospital commander. The other is a personal choice. Not surprisingly, I asked my father to do the honors. He was smiling from ear to ear as he pinned the bright brass oak leaf on my shoulder.

My apprehension regarding the move to Alabama had been unfounded. I was happy to sell our house but sad to go. Anniston had given me such a different experience than I expected. Had the world changed so much? Was my feeling of being an outcast and not being equal all inside of me?

I began to think that the worst was over.

CHAPTER 12

CAREFUL WHAT YOU WISH FOR

On my way to Fort Meade in mid-July, I stopped at my parents' house in Richmond. My father was slowly recovering from bypass surgery, and he was weak. He had little appetite and had lost a lot of weight. My mother was still giving him hemodialysis treatments at home, but because his stamina varied from day to day, it was difficult for him to plan his schedule. As drained as he was, he still asked that I leave the girls with them for a few days. He said having Hannah and Amal in the house boosted his morale. This would give me the opportunity to sign in at Fort Meade, get in-processed, and get settled in new housing, so I agreed to let the girls stay with my parents.

Fort Meade, in Anne Arundel County, Maryland, is a small city in and of itself. The National Security Agency, a separate entity, lies within its boundaries. The decision to live on-post was an easy one—anything we would need was close by. There was a huge post exchange (PX) comparable to a department store. There was a gas station, a library, and a commissary. All the necessary facilities for health and fitness were onsite as well, including a hospital, medical and dental clinics, and a large, well-equipped gym. Having easy access to all these amenities saved a lot of time, especially since the traffic in the Baltimore/DC area can be so bad that running errands is an ordeal.

Fort Meade also had its own schools. I enrolled the girls in Pershing Hill Elementary School, two blocks from our quarters. With Hannah almost eight and Amal six, they could walk there on their own. As had been the case at Fort McClellan, my day started with PT at 5:00 a.m. followed by the usual morning weekday routine. Hannah carried the house key; she was in charge of locking the door when they left for school and letting themselves back into the house after they walked home. They were the quintessential latchkey kids.

My daughters were now old enough to ask questions about our nation's history. Unlike their father, who often told me how much he hated the United States, I was an unabashed patriot from the time I was a girl. I still get emotional whenever I hear "The Star-Spangled Banner."

I made a point of taking the girls to see landmarks like the Lincoln Memorial, the Library of Congress, the Supreme Court, and the White House. This proved to be a tough balancing act because I also wanted to visit my parents as often as I could. They were, after all, the reason why I had requested a transfer from Fort McClellan.

Whenever we went to Richmond, my father's eyes lit up as soon as the girls and I walked through the door. His love for us seemed to emanate from every part of him. My mother still greeted us without emotion, but she always had a hearty meal ready. Hannah and Amal loved their visits with Oma and Opa, and they usually presented them with crayon artwork when we arrived.

My unit at Fort Meade, Kimbrough Army Community Hospital, was a small 36-bed facility, but it didn't have anything like the warm, collegial atmosphere that I'd enjoyed so much at Fort

McClellan. Major Alice Hayes was my sponsor. She was a short, stocky, and plain-faced woman with a blunt, forceful persona entirely devoid of compassion. She was also my supervisor—all Army, all the time. She didn't care about my personal life or about anyone's personal life, for that matter. Surreptitiously, nurses who worked with her called her "Alice Malice."

At our initial meeting, all she wanted to know was how soon I could get to work. She was irritated at having to wait until I had finished in-processing, and as soon as I started, she really piled it on. I was swamped from day one.

Earlier in the summer, while the girls were in Kokomo with Nadir, I spent two weeks at Fort Sam in San Antonio to take the Army's head nurse course. Little did I know I'd be putting my new skill set to work so soon. Although I had transferred in as the clinic's OB/GYN NP, Alice Malice also made me interim head nurse. The previous head nurse, a civilian, had been relieved of her duties (in plain English, she was fired) and it didn't take me long to figure out why. She had left behind a two-year accumulation of unevaluated patient PAP smears and other lab results. How many were abnormal? Nobody knew.

Major Hayes saddled me with the job of reviewing them and notifying any patients who had abnormal results. Because there had already been such a lengthy delay, these women needed follow-up medical attention as quickly as possible, but for me, it was a huge load of extra work. This paperwork mountain was perched on top of my already-packed schedule of gynecological, obstetrical, and postpartum patients, along with any other administrative duties I had as head nurse.

Alice Malice was unconcerned. "I don't care how much time you put into it, just get it done as fast as you can," she said.

The only way I could do that was to work after hours but the clinic closed at 4:30 p.m. and I had to get home to my girls. To manage the problem, I elected to take the backlog home so I could work on it after Hannah and Amal went to bed. I put the gigantic pile in order by date, starting with the oldest, and began going over the lab results.

I was whittling the pile down, but Alice Malice was as impatient as she was disagreeable. She immediately began hounding me about it, asking me daily how soon I'd be finished. I always gave her the same answer: "I'm working on it a little each day."

Her relentless questioning annoyed me. Then she noted that I always left the clinic at 4:30 p.m. "How are you getting these labs done if you're leaving work when the clinic closes—or are you simply putting it off?" she asked.

"I take it all home," I replied, trying to keep my cool. "I've been working on it in the evenings after my children are asleep."

"You can't do that!" she snapped. "Those are official government documents that have private patient information on them! You cannot take them home with you!"

I was thrown off by the harshness of her response but did my best not to show it. "I live on post in government quarters, and no one looks at them but me," I replied evenly. "I'm a single parent. It's the only way I can get this done and take care of my children."

"Your children, your children, your children. Your father, your father, your father," Alice Malice barked. "This is the Army! Your job comes first, children or no children!"

"Yes, ma'am," I answered calmly. I knew better than to talk back to her. She seemed to take particular delight in being cruel—to me, she was the second coming of Nurse Ratchet from *One Flew Over the Cuckoo's Nest*.

Inside my head and behind my serene straight face, I was screaming at her as loud as I could. *You coldhearted, meanspirit-*

ed, miserable bitch! I yelled to myself. *I'm here because I requested compassionate reassignment, and I'm not going to sacrifice my time with my daughters or with my parents because you dumped this pile of shit on me! This backlog is your fault—you weren't paying attention when the last head nurse screwed up, which is how it got this big. You could've worked on it yourself or split the workload with me, but instead, you stuck me with all of it.*

I continued to smuggle the paperwork home with me. It took me several weeks but I got it done. It was almost a year before the position of head nurse was filled. Finally, relieved of my time-consuming administrative duties, I could at last focus on my work as an NP. Providing excellent OB/GYN care was my calling, the job I had come to love. The women I saw at Kimbrough, like most women, tended to put themselves last. For many of my patients, their annual GYN visit was the only time they got a thorough exam and a chance to speak with a medical professional. For me as their NP, this meant not only checking their reproductive health but also talking with them and "listening between the lines" to see if they had other health problems that needed to be addressed.

My clinic schedule was busy, and even though we provided complete prenatal and postpartum care, we had some significant logistical challenges with our OB patients. Fort Meade had its own hospital, but it didn't have a maternity ward, so our mothers-to-be had to go to WRAMC to give birth. Each time I saw my patients, I made sure to remind them to head for Walter Reed when they went into labor. I also told them not to dawdle. Babies about to be born can be impatient, and the trip to WRAMC could take an hour or more, sometimes a lot more. Not all my patients heeded the warnings, and I did manage to deliver a baby in an ambulance when we were stuck in heavy Beltway traffic and didn't make it to the hospital in time.

During this time, my father strongly encouraged me to continue working toward a master's degree. He'd often tell me, "*Yalla, shed-e-haelik,*" which in Arabic basically means, "Come on, pick yourself up." He knew I'd need a master's degree to be competitive for the next promotion to lieutenant colonel. I soon registered for an evening class in statistics and probability at the University of Maryland.

* * * * *

Meanwhile, Nadir's child support payments stopped altogether. I was still fighting him for the money I needed to take care of the girls—money to which I was legally entitled. In early November 1986, I received a notice from the court in Indiana that I was to appear in person for a hearing on the 25th of the month.

Not again, I thought. I doubted whether it was absolutely necessary to be there in person, but when I called my attorney, he told me I had to appear. The day before the hearing, I packed up Hannah and Amal and took off for Kokomo.

We stayed with Sarah and Lawrie. Out of earshot of the girls, Sarah filled me in on the turmoil that had taken place next door. Nadir had apparently auctioned off the house and all its contents and then disappeared without his wife and young daughters. Before that happened, however, Miriam had become a frequent visitor at Sarah and Lawrie's house "to get away from *him*!" Sarah exclaimed. "And Mona," she added, "what she told me sounded a lot like what you'd said a few years ago. The stories sounded *very* familiar." She paused. "You know, Mona, I have to admit…when you told me what was going on, I'm afraid I didn't quite believe you. Then Miriam began telling me the exact same thing. Forgive me for doubting you."

"There's nothing to forgive, Sarah," I replied. "Whether you believed me or not, I received nothing but love and kindness from you and Lawrie every time I knocked on your door. And in retrospect, I can see how some of it would sound pretty farfetched."

"One day, Miriam came to see me with a *very* personal question," Sarah began, then paused again. It looked like she was unsure whether or not to continue. "She asked me whether I knew a women's surgeon...someone who could make her a new hymen—like a virgin. I would never have believed that someone would actually ask a question like that if I didn't *hear* it *myself,* Mona."

I believed it immediately, and I also knew it wasn't Miriam's idea. This was what Nadir wanted. He had suggested it to me, too, as part of his relentless effort to destroy my self-esteem. He had tried to brand me as "used up, like a piece of old furniture that nobody wants."

As Sarah was talking, I realized yet again how fortunate I was to have the support of my family when I made the decision to leave Nadir. I thought of how dismal my life had been and all the shit Nadir dished out to me over the years, both when we were married and after the divorce. I felt blessed to be free of him and wondered how Miriam was managing.

"What about Miriam and her three little ones? Where did they go?" I asked Sarah with concern.

"I think some people from a mosque in Indianapolis helped them," Sarah explained. "I really don't know for sure."

I felt sorry for Miriam. She arrived in Indiana speaking no English, married to a man who was a near-stranger. She came with no knowledge of the culture and without friends or family to support her. Still, she had a kind heart, and she'd taken care of my girls as she had said she would. After bearing three daughters, she'd become a prisoner in her own home, entirely at the mercy of her abusive husband. Miriam didn't deserve that. No woman does.

When I went to court the next day, my attorney met me. Nadir's lawyer appeared and informed the court that he was withdrawing from the case because his client had left the country to take up residence in Egypt.

This didn't make sense to me. Even if Nadir left the country, I was quite sure he wouldn't have gone to Egypt. As soon as he returned there, he would've been conscripted into the military. To repay his government loans—the money he had used to begin his studies at Berkeley—he would've been required to serve at least two years in the Egyptian Army. It was the commitment he made when he accepted his student visa, but during the time we were married, Nadir repeatedly and adamantly told me he had no intention of honoring it. Now that he had his PhD and his American citizenship, I couldn't imagine that he'd changed his mind. My guess was that he'd lied to his lawyer, the same way he lied to everyone else.

Years later, I learned that Nadir married yet again, another Egyptian woman, and had purchased a home in Delaware near his brother, Sammon. His new wife bore him two sons. He eventually took a university position in Saudi Arabia. This was a strategic move on his part—he relocated to a country where he wouldn't be obligated to pay court-ordered child support for his five daughters.

I never heard from Nadir again. Neither did Hannah and Amal. The girls took it in stride. I'd always been honest with them about what kind of man Nadir was, and they'd certainly seen enough for themselves during their month-long stays in Kokomo. The girls didn't miss him because you can't miss someone who was never really in your life to begin with.

In the end, Nadir turned out to be the "mother" of all deadbeat dads.

His departure didn't change a thing. I continued to raise my daughters and pursue my career as an Army nurse. I applied for the Army's long-term civilian training program, which would allow me to attend graduate school while still receiving full pay and benefits. In early 1987, I was accepted at the University of Texas Health Science Center in San Antonio for a program leading to a master's degree in women's health care. *Alhamdulillah!*

That happy news was offset by my father's ongoing decline, which soon made it impossible for him to keep working. When he retired, my parents moved to Manhattan, Kansas where my older brother Rick now lived with his family. Rick had only been there a year, having just moved after he completed his medical residency in California.

THE PHYSICAL DRAIN TAKES ITS TOLL

By this time, I was exhausted —the stresses of trying to juggle work, school, and parenting had worn me down. On top of that, I was drained from years of battling Nadir for child support and from driving to Richmond to be with my parents on weekends. It had all started to take a toll on my health, and a few weeks after my parents moved, I became increasingly debilitated, barely able to take care of my daughters. A lengthy visit to their Uncle Rick and Auntie Barbara, where they were enrolled in school for the rest of the school year, helped me recover. The added advantage was that this was the perfect opportunity for Hannah and Amal to bond more with their cousins.

I was incapacitated—in and out of the hospital and convalescent leave—for much of the spring and into the summer. Eventually, I was diagnosed with an intestinal amoebic infection and meningitis. After treatment with intravenous and oral antibiotics followed by bed rest at home, I felt well enough in July to move to San Antonio to begin my graduate studies. I rushed to clear out my quarters, packed my car, and made a beeline for Manhattan to pick up the girls, which was another 12-hour drive. Then we all journeyed to San Antonio for a new beginning.

CHAPTER 13

ANOTHER WINDOW OPENS

I started graduate school in August 1987. The women's health-care graduate program was designed to prepare the student to be either a clinical nurse specialist or an NP. There were seven students in the entire class. Two of us were active duty, two were married to active-duty officers, and three were civilians. The program was intense with lots of reading, papers, projects, and exams. In addition, we all had to complete a comprehensive research project. HIV and AIDS were relatively new diseases, and I chose to examine that topic, specifically with respect to how it affects women, pregnancy, and newborns.

In the early months of 1988 my parents had moved back to California. Vati was subsequently hospitalized several times for problems with his arteriovenous fistula, the port through which he received dialysis. He came down with pneumonia and had excess fluid drained from his chest cavity twice. Each time he was discharged, he returned home weaker than before. In April, he fell—this time he fractured his right hip.

After the surgery, he needed a walker to get around and was never quite the same. By May, Mutti told me he was having episodes of cognitive impairment, and they were happening with increasing frequency. He went in and out of reality—as if there were venetian blinds on his brain. He'd hallucinate, picking at his bedsheets, convinced there were ants crawling all over him. He was soon readmitted to the hospital because his doctor suspected that the incision in his hip was infected. The infection, coupled with persistent pneumonia, was potentially life-threatening.

In June, the girls and I drove to Fresno to see him at the hospital. Vati obviously no longer remembered that I was in graduate school. When he began babbling words I couldn't decipher, Hannah and Amal were visibly shaken. Nevertheless, they approached his bed, one on each side, to hold his hand and give him a kiss on his cheek. I was relieved that he recognized them and responded to their tenderness. It gripped my heart and soul to see my dear father in such a diminished state. He had always been this giant of a man, not physically, but emotionally and intellectually, and now he seemed so fragile, so vulnerable.

"Mommy, is Opa all right?" Hannah asked with genuine concern.

An innocent question from an innocent child, but my words died in my throat as I began to answer. I had always tried to tell my daughters the truth, but now I struggled with the thoughts and emotions that were battling in my brain. The cool voice of reason and logic kept insisting that I look at the situation like the experienced nurse that I was—if the man in that hospital bed hadn't been my father, my judgment as a healthcare professional would be that his prognosis was poor.

But it *was* my father, and a tidal wave of denial quickly rushed in to drown out my reality-based clinical assessment. *Vati couldn't possibly be dying,* I told myself. He was too young to leave us now. He was such a benevolent being, a devoted father and grandfather.

He had so much love to give and so much to teach his grand-children. We needed him. The grandchildren needed him. We all needed his love so desperately. *Have a little faith*, my heart said to my head. *Of course he'll get better.*

After two weeks in the hospital, Vati did actually begin to improve. How much would he recover? His doctor said that would depend on getting his multiple infections under control. When he was discharged, I returned to San Antonio because I was enrolled in the six-week summer session. At Vati's request, I allowed Hannah and Amal to stay in Fresno—it was summer vacation for them anyway.

I'd been back in San Antonio for two weeks when I had a terrible dream. I heard my father calling out to me, "Mona, Mona, *ya habibti*, Mona." The dream frightened me awake, and when I opened my eyes, my pillow was soaked with my tears. I was crying for my father, for his suffering, for the fact that medical science could do so little for him now.

It was an omen. As I was trying to go back to sleep, the phone rang. "It's your father, Mona, you better come to Fresno. Vati just passed away." Goosebumps covered my body as I heard my mother's stoic voice. The room spun around me. *Am I still dreaming*, I wondered. *Or is this reality?*

Vati's condition had bottomed out—his hip incision still wasn't healing and he was bleeding profusely. When his blood pressure dropped severely, he lost consciousness. Paramedics were called, and he was taken by ambulance to the hospital where he was pronounced dead on arrival. I took the first flight I could get.

THE FUNERAL

Vati's funeral was to be a traditional Islamic funeral. No one in the family, including me, knew much about the protocols and rituals of Muslim burials, and we didn't have much time to learn. In the Islamic faith, interment should take place as soon as possible after death, preferably within 24 hours. We planned Vati's funeral based on the information we received from the members of the local Islamic center but even that wasn't much to go on.

In preparation for burial, there is an essential ritual, *ghusl*, that entails bathing the body, and it is generally performed by close relatives of the same gender as the deceased. Following *ghusl*, the body is enshrouded in plain white cotton or linen cloth then placed into the casket. Family members, friends, and other Muslims of the community then gather to offer their collective prayers for the forgiveness of the deceased. This is the *Salat al-Janazah*, or funeral prayer. Vati had friends of all faiths, and many of those who came to his funeral to pay their last respects were not Muslim. We invited them to offer prayers in accordance with their own beliefs.

Our old neighbors, Andy and Betty Johnson, came all the way from St. Louis to see us as did the Guerrero family from Hawthorne. Dearest Ed and Leona were there as well. We all reminisced about Vati and celebrated his life and his legacy.

For the funeral, Islamic custom dictated that I wear black clothing and cover my hair, and I had no issue with this tradition. What happened next, however, brought me into direct confrontation with the imam who was leading the service. It was the same imam who had conducted my brother Rick's marriage and then told me my signature as a witness was half as legitimate as the signature of a man.

"You have to stand in the back, behind the men," he said as he tried to guide me away from the grave. Looking over my shoulder, I saw all the other women, including my mother, standing meekly behind the male mourners.

I shook my head. "Thank you, but I'm going to stay here, next to my brothers," I replied firmly.

"In Islam, women are to remain in the back of the burial site," the *imam* intoned, as if his declaration alone could make me move.

All it did was annoy me. "Why?" I asked. "What difference does it make?"

"Women tend to cry and let their emotions take over," he said. "Maybe they will throw themselves into the grave or behave in some other unseemly manner, causing great distraction and interrupting the solemnity of the service."

Are you fucking kidding me? Did he really believe I'd accept his overblown, cartoon mischaracterization of women's emotions and behavior? I'm a major in the US Army! It would have been ridiculous if it hadn't been so condescending. Either way, I wasn't going to dignify such drivel with a response. I just stared at him. I also stood my ground.

The night before, my mother and I had gone over the funeral arrangements while my brothers and other male members of the Islamic center bathed and prepared my father's body for burial. During that time and at various intervals, my mother and I cried—and so did my brothers.

We cried together and comforted one another—that's what families do when they've lost a loved one. It made no logical sense to me to separate family members at the gravesite. I couldn't find a reference in the Qur'an about where a woman's presence at a burial site should be. Even more so, I was angry at the imam's highhanded efforts to order me around. Who was he to deprive me of the right to bid farewell to my father as I saw fit and in the same manner as my brothers? This was *my* father.

"It's forbidden for women to come this close to the gravesite," the imam said once more.

I looked over my shoulder again. The rest of the women were still standing at the rear, except my mother who was making her way to where I was standing near the front.

"Just do as he says, Mona," Mutti pleaded. "You're creating a scene."

I believed I was doing something else entirely. As far as I was concerned, I was doing what I'd been brought up to do—to hold my own in the face of prejudice and in the face of unreasonable rules and regulations.

I'd learned this not only from Vati but from Mutti herself. My mother was the one who drew a bright line between archaic Islamic traditions that were rooted in male-dominated custom and what the Qur'an actually declared. It was Mutti who took on a small gang of religious zealots in Dhahran when they tried to flog her because she wasn't wearing an abaya.

And it was Vati who made sure I had the same opportunity as my brothers. From the time I was a little girl, my father always told me I could do anything that boys could do. I never doubted that he loved and valued me, just as he loved and valued his sons. After all, when he realized that even the school for the daughters of the Saudi royal family would provide me with nothing more than a third-grade education, we left Dhahran for Los Angeles and a new beginning. He had brought us to America not only in search of a better life for us all but specifically in search of a better future *for me*.

My father gave me the greatest gifts anyone can receive—unconditional love and the right to control my own destiny. He was the one who protected me and stood up for me when I was a little girl, cowering from my mother's spankings. While I was in school and especially when we lived in St. Louis, he was my primary defender against bigotry and intolerance. While Vati was culturally traditional in many ways, he was by all means very progressive compared to most Muslim fathers when it came to a daughter's well-being. How truly blessed I was.

His unwavering love and support was a constant reminder that I had a purpose on this earth, a purpose that could only be fulfilled with a good education. And now because of that education and what I had learned about US history, I felt as if being ordered to the back of the gravesite meant exactly the same thing as being ordered to the back of the bus. And like Mutti in Dhahran, I wasn't having it.

"With all due respect, sir," I replied, "I'm staying here."

The dichotomy between my Muslim heritage and my American sensibilities as an empowered adult woman had never been so raw, so painful. The imam glowered at me, but I stayed put as he began the ritual prayers.

After the prayers were over, my brothers and other male members of the Islamic center slowly lowered the casket into the grave. Then in the customary manner, each of us picked up a handful of soil and threw it into the grave while reciting, "We were created from soil and we return you back into it." As the gravediggers began to cover the casket, final prayers were recited in unison. Once the funeral service was over, neither my mother nor my brothers spoke of the confrontation between the imam and me. To them, it was as if it had never happened, and I never looked back.

At that moment, I finally felt equal.

CHAPTER 14

ON TO WEST GERMANY

My assignment upon graduation was at the 97th General Hospital (GH) in Frankfurt, West Germany. I knew this would be different right from the beginning when Colonel Ronald Blanck, the commanding officer (CO), called all five of us new officers in for a meeting. We gathered around his desk as he welcomed us and briefed us on what to expect. He then asked that we each tell a bit about ourselves and our backgrounds. None of my previous commanding officers had ever done this.

Captain Phillip Rice was sitting opposite from me. As I described my background as an NP and briefly my family history, he looked at me with particular interest and curiosity.

He smiled, and there seemed to be a spark between us that flew across the room, just like in the movies.

Phil had sandy blond hair, a well-groomed mustache, and sky-blue eyes that sparkled through wire-rimmed glasses. He had recently completed his graduate school program in nurse anesthesia at Texas Wesleyan University. His gentle tone and unassuming nature reminded me of my father.

It was January 1989, the twilight of the Cold War, and Germany was still divided. Although the two countries were adjacent to one another, they were worlds apart. West Germany was a prosperous and independent democracy. East Germany was an impoverished Soviet client state. Its consumers faced chronic shortages of everything, including light bulbs and toilet paper, and it was becoming all but impossible for the repressive regime to keep its citizens in the dark about how much better life was in West Germany. The border between the two countries was heavily militarized, ostensibly to stop West Germany and its NATO allies from invading the East. In reality, however, the biggest job of the East German (and Soviet) military was to keep their own people from fleeing in search of a better life.

I instantly became enamored with Frankfurt. The city had a tremendous amount of vitality. With Berlin surrounded by East Germany, Frankfurt had become West Germany's financial and banking capital, as well as its transportation hub. The 97th GH was in the middle of this conventional modern city. Combined with its 11 outlying clinics throughout the greater Frankfurt area, it was also referred to as the Frankfurt Army Regional Medical Center (FARMC) and was the Army's largest medical facility outside the US. Several years after being posted there, the 97th GH closed its doors. The buildings today serve as the US Consulate General.

Colonel Blanck fostered a high level of professionalism and camaraderie. Thanks to him and to our chief nurse, Colonel Nancy Adams, we were able to provide top-notch care in a collegial atmosphere. We worked together as a team, encouraging, mentoring, and supporting each other. In the OB/GYN clinic, we had several doctors, four midwives, and me, the NP. Because the civilian head nurse position was vacant when I arrived, I once again had to fulfill those duties as well.

In addition to the usual in-processing procedures, all soldiers newly posted to Frankfurt were required to take a two-week course in German language and culture. Since I already knew German, this was a breeze for me. I also took a driving class so I could get a European driver's license, and I had my car shipped to Frankfurt from the States.

In-processing also included a series of Subversion and Espionage Directed at the Army (SAEDA) briefings so we had better awareness of the threats and dangers of the Cold War. We were presented with various scenarios to teach us how to recognize the many forms these potentially dangerous activities could take. These briefings also served to remind us that we were all ambassadors for the US and were to conduct ourselves accordingly.

Housing in West Germany was a bit more complicated than it had been back home. Army regulation dictated that I couldn't receive travel orders for my dependents until I had adequate housing available, so Hannah and Amal remained in Fresno. I had the option to either live on-post or in the surrounding German community. I wanted my daughters to go to local German schools and be immersed in German culture, and I was hopeful they would learn the language quickly, the same way I had learned English as a girl. If I lived on post and they attended the American school, it'd be near-impossible for this to happen.

My temporary quarters turned out to be a room at the Ambassador Hotel on post, but as soon as my car arrived, I drove out to explore various communities suggested by the housing office. About 12 miles northeast of Frankfurt was a little town called Klein Karben. After I checked out the local elementary school, I decided to take a lease on one of eight new townhouses all set in a row. As one of the first occupants, I got to choose the corner unit, which had a larger yard and better lighting. The good news was that everything was brand new; the bad news was that in Germany, "everything" didn't include standard features that were always part of a home in the US. My new residence had no kitchen or bathroom cabinets. No faucets, toilets, sinks, closets, or light fixtures.

The house was a shell. I was disconcerted by the prospect of becoming my own building contractor, seeing as I'd have to buy and install toilets, bathroom and kitchen sinks, and cabinets. Fortunately, I was not the first officer to face this problem. The Army's housing office had dealt with this before and arranged to install everything I needed to move in. I had a telephone connected as soon as I signed the lease to call Mutti and the girls. I took the opportunity to call my aunt in Switzerland as well as other relatives living in West Germany. While I was in Europe, I intended to take advantage of my time to travel. I wanted to see the continent and above all to see my family members whom I'd either never met or hadn't seen in years.

A few weeks later, my new home was ready to move into. While I was transferring some personal belongings from the Ambassador Hotel to my new quarters, I ran into Phil, who had leased the townhouse at the other end of the complex. That's when I caught myself being happy. Some might call it happenstance but I was never much of a believer in coincidence. Whatever it was, the idea that we would be neighbors made me very glad indeed.

I ran into Phil again at a SAEDA briefing the following week. I told him about my aunt and mentioned that she had some furniture to give me. These were pieces that I wanted because they had belonged to my grandmother. My problem was figuring out how to get them back to my townhouse. Phil's face brightened up immediately. His car, which was actually a van, had just arrived from the US, and he suggested that we could drive together to Lugano, visit my aunt and uncle, then load up the van and drive back with the furniture. I was surprised by his generous offer and immediately accepted.

Lugano is almost 400 miles south of Frankfurt. We arrived at Tante Aidi's home about seven hours after we left Frankfurt. Her new house was astonishing—I'd never seen it before. When I'd visited with the girls three years earlier, she and Francis had told me they were going to build a new home over Francis' atelier. The large, light-filled living space had windows all around and a panoramic view of the meadows below. With Onkel Francis' finest paintings framed and hanging on the walls, it felt as if they were living inside a modern art museum.

Tante Aidi fussed over us. She always went out of her way to prepare delicious meals, and conversation was stimulating, even as it ping-ponged back and forth between German and English.

When Tante Aidi and I were alone together, I confided to her—in German—that I was attracted to Phil. "I don't know him that well, at least not yet, but..." I said.

She gave me a nod and a knowing smile. Over the years, we had kept in touch through letters, telephone calls, and intermittent visits back and forth. After my separation from Nadir, I visited her every few years, taking my daughters with me, as I wanted her to be a role model for them. I relied on her evolved, practical, and innovative thinking whenever I needed a confidant. Throughout the years, she had given me sound and objective advice, and now I was seeking it once more.

"It's chemistry, my dear, chemistry!" she said. "He seems very *sympathisch*. Regardless of who gives you guidance, ultimately you must follow your heart."

Phil and I carefully loaded the furniture into the van before leaving to return to Frankfurt. There weren't many items: A square breakfast table with four chairs, two small bookcases, three occasional tables, and a lamp. I looked forward to having the pieces in my home, not just because I'd be able to use them but because it would be like having a bit of my grandmother's memory with me every day. Phil and I talked all the way back to Frankfurt, just as we had on the way to Lugano.

As the weeks went by, Phil and I established a connection. Unlike my relationships with other men where I always had to be cautious, on guard, and mindful of my safety, I felt comfortable with Phil. I felt safe. I felt heard when I spoke. Best of all, I felt like I could be myself without fear of being chided, criticized, browbeaten, ignored, or otherwise mistreated. I truly felt like his equal in our relationship. As we became better acquainted and spent more time together, I felt a deep sense of friendship.

But there was also something more. Whenever I thought about Phil or was in his presence, I felt butterflies in my belly. It took me a little bit to realize what this unfamiliar fluttering was. For the first time in my life, at the age of 37, I was in love. Head over heels.

I was thrilled when my household goods were delivered, and overjoyed when I received travel orders authorizing me to fly to Fresno to bring Hannah and Amal to Germany. Finally! It had been six months since I'd seen them and I'd missed them so. This was the longest we'd ever been separated.

At their German elementary school, the girls were something of a novelty as the only Americans. Within a few short months, their knowledge of the German language blossomed, and they began walking to and from school with their new pals, chattering away just like the locals.

A Surprise During Mail Call

Everyone in the Army posted overseas has an Army post office (APO) address. To facilitate mail communication with family, friends, and business contacts, military personnel send and receive mail using US postage, same as they would if they were stateside.

At the 97th GH, our post office was located inside the hospital. In early fall of 1989, the mailroom attendant handed me a small package with an Antwerp return address. But I didn't know anyone in Belgium.

As soon as I returned to my clinic, I opened it—and let out a huge shriek of joy. The package contained a ring with a large diamond. It fit perfectly. This was Phil's charming and romantic way of asking me to be his wife. I was thrilled, and those butterflies fluttered like never before. It was the autumn of 1989, right before the fall of the Berlin Wall.

Much as I wanted to, I couldn't share this moment with Phil, who was in the operating room administering anesthesia to a patient. When I peered through the window of the OR to catch his attention, I nodded "yes" and waved my left hand at him so he could see the sparkle. His mouth and nose were covered by his surgical mask but the glow in his eyes was unmistakable.

I spent the rest of the day on cloud nine.

East Berlin

Official travel information came from our command, mostly about places to avoid, but our best intel came from word of mouth. Many soldiers posted to Frankfurt traveled and everyone was willing to share tips and recommendations. The prevailing wisdom at the 97th GH was that East Berlin was a must-see destination. Getting there, however, took some doing; travel to East Berlin required flag orders, which had to be requested and approved two to three weeks in advance.

Flag orders were emblazoned with the Stars and Stripes at the top of each page and had been around since the end of World War II. They identified US Army personnel as members of the Allies, the winning side, for the purposes of crossing from sector to sector in divided, conquered Germany. Because the US had never formally recognized East Germany as a sovereign nation, as far as the American military was concerned, East Germany and its capital, East Berlin, were under the control of the Soviet Union.

I drove to East Berlin with two other American women twice and once by duty train with family and visitors. To get to East Berlin from Frankfurt, one had to enter the Soviet sector, traverse it, enter West Berlin, and then enter East Berlin. This meant three border crossings with three checkpoints and three exasperating encounters with Soviet bureaucracy.

Checkpoint Alpha at Marienborn/Helmstedt was a glorified wooden shack. The 1950s décor was tacky and like the shack itself, it had seen better days. Two couches—one threadbare tangerine, the other lumpy grey—faced one another on opposite walls. Faded portraits of Marx, Lenin, and Stalin hung above the couches. Everything was drab, and the dim light made it even more grungy and depressing than it already was.

Whoever was manning the checkpoint sat behind a large sliding glass window. There was no way to know what this individual looked like because most of his head was hidden by a roller shade. All I could see was a nose and mouth, but I figured it was a guy when the window slid open and a hairy hand emerged. "Papers, please," said the mouth in a heavy Russian accent. I handed the flag orders, my ID, and the two passports of my companions to the hairy hand, which then closed the window. After 30 minutes and a great deal of paper shuffling and energetic rubber stamping, the window slid open again. "What is the intention of your visit?" the mouth asked. His English was barely intelligible, but I knew the answer because the Army had briefed us on what to say: "To go to Berlin." Without another word, the hairy hand initialed the forms, entered the time of day, and slid the window shut. It all felt so clandestine, like an old spy movie or a John le Carré novel.

On the way out, we passed a table of propaganda leaflets in both English and German that pledged that "Communism is good for the people," but we still weren't free to go. Another Russian soldier was inspecting the car. Once he was satisfied that there was nothing suspicious about the vehicle itself, he sketched a diagram on my flag orders indicating how much gas there was in the tank. He also wrote down the mileage on the odometer and the time we departed Checkpoint Alpha.

Checkpoint Bravo was 110 miles further east. When we got there, we had to repeat the same process again. Before we were permitted to leave East Germany and enter West Berlin, my flag orders were stamped and our arrival time was noted. This was crucial: At Checkpoint Alpha, we'd been given a 2.5- to 3-hour window to get to Bravo and going too fast was as bad as too slow. One meant we'd been speeding through the People's Republic and the other would cause them to suspect we were spies who had taken an unauthorized detour.

After entering West Berlin, we reached Friedrich Strasse and arrived at the infamous Checkpoint Charlie where we would cross the Berlin Wall. The west side of the wall was decorated with colorful graffiti art. The east side, however, was a no-man's land that was punctuated by occasional guard towers. Known as the death strip, it was patrolled by grim-faced, heavily armed soldiers. Their mission was to prevent their countrymen from fleeing, using lethal force if necessary.

The reasons why anyone would try to leave were obvious: Crossing into East Berlin was like going back 40 years. Theoretically, it was still 1950 in East Berlin.

The buildings were bigger, more urban versions of the shack at Checkpoint Alpha, and they were drab and poorly maintained. The same went for the cars on the streets, which came in only three flavors: One Russian (the Lada) and two East German (the Wartburg and Trabant, or Trabi). The German cars, the Trabis in particular, looked flimsy and unreliable. They had plastic bodies, anemic two-cylinder engines, and tailpipes that belched huge clouds of black exhaust. Trabis had virtually no safety features— like everything else in East Germany, they'd changed little since 1950.

I was struck by the personalities of the people, or rather their lack of personality. They were polite but went about their business without enthusiasm. There was no animation in their gestures, no inflection in their voices. Their eyes had no lively sparkle. In psychological terms, they had what would be called a "flat affect." In pop-culture terms, they looked like zombies.

In their zeal to establish universal equality, the Communists had eradicated any rationale for individual initiative. Every adult had a job, albeit at poverty wages. Worst of all, there was no escape. My heart went out to the people of East Berlin. They were stuck in this life and it was a terrible life to be stuck in. It was the same when we traveled to Czechoslovakia and was no different in other countries of the Eastern Bloc.

Phil and I traveled all over Europe, including Denmark, Switzerland, Sweden, France, Belgium, Czechoslovakia, and Turkey. Sometimes we went alone, but more often we took the girls with us and traveled together as a family. When we traveled to Turkey, we went by military hop, a huge C-5 cargo plane. Hannah and Amal were the only kids on board, and the crew members were so smitten with them that they took them to the cockpit and allowed them to "steer and fly" the plane.

CHAPTER 15

THE WAR ON MY CULTURE

On the night of January 17, 1991, my brother, Rick, called me. It was the first time I'd spoken to him in several months. "Are you okay?" he asked.

He had good reason to ask. In response to Saddam Hussein's attempt to seize Kuwait, thereby threatening Saudi Arabia, the full force of US air power was raining bombs on Baghdad. Operation Desert Storm—the Gulf War—had begun.

Rick asked if there was anything I needed, anything he could do to help. "Just tell everyone I love them," I said, meaning our mother and brothers and their families. We ended the conversation on a positive note, and I felt Rick's full love and support.

The preceding months had been hectic for us at the 97th GH. In late summer of 1990, Iraq invaded and occupied neighboring Kuwait, putting Iraqi military forces within striking distance of Saudi oil fields. Some sort of US response had been widely anticipated but that was as much as we knew. After being ordered to plan for incoming wounded, the hospital hurriedly expanded our capacity, relocating our clinics and offices to make room. Additional beds, linens, medical equipment, and supplies that had been stockpiled throughout Europe were sent to the 97th GH. All elective surgeries were canceled or postponed, and although we continued to care for our pregnant women and postpartum outpatients, we began referring women in their ninth month or those in labor to local German civilian hospitals to give birth.

Anticipating a wave of battle casualties, my supervisor put me in charge of orienting the reserve nurses assigned to our department. If we received Saudi patients, I was to assist with their triage and translate from Arabic to English for my colleagues. Phil was as busy as I was—all the operating rooms and recovery rooms had been double and triple staffed. We all felt ready and fully prepared to accept whatever was coming our way. We remained calm and professional, even as we worried about how the crisis would be resolved.

As hectic as it was at work, Phil and I tried to keep it business as usual at home: School, family meals, time with friends. We deliberately didn't talk with Hannah and Amal about our fevered preparations for an influx of the wounded. I didn't want to frighten the girls, and I especially didn't want them to stress about the possibility of another separation. If I were to be redeployed, there was a possibility that I'd have to send them back to the States to live with Rick and his family in Kansas. I was hoping it wouldn't come to that, but then again, I'd been hoping it wouldn't come to this either. And yet here we were at war with Iraq.

War…As the air offensive against Saddam Hussein began, I thought a lot about how we Americans have come to describe sending troops into battle. Up until Vietnam, we called it what it was—war. But since then, it seemed to me that whenever the US military referred to armed combat, our leaders found softer, less offensive words to describe it: A campaign, a strike, an operation, an offensive, a police action, even a peacekeeping mission. But we seldom called it "war." And our press reported it the same way.

As far as the wounded were concerned, it was a distinction without a difference. Whatever euphemism the politicians and the media used, their blood was just as red, their pain just as real, their lives just as shattered. Even though I was loyal to our nation and our military, I often felt like "we the people" were getting played a bit by the way these actions were sold to the public to gain their support.

On the night the bombing began, I was finally home after a long, hard day at the clinic. The girls were settled in for the night, homework completed, and ready for school the next morning. Phil and I were watching the German nightly news on TV. We could see that our bombs were still falling on Iraq as they had been all day.

All that ordnance falling from the sky lit up the city of Baghdad like a July Fourth celebration. On the ground, there was nothing to celebrate, and I began crying uncontrollably. Phil asked me several times why I was having such an intense emotional reaction. He tried to reassure me that we were safe and far removed from danger, both physically and emotionally.

But I wasn't crying for me. I was crying for the innocent citizens on the ground. My tears were not for the Iraqi military or government or for their bombastic, psychologically unstable president, but for people—many of them women and children—cowering in fear as the bombs continued to fall.

I was also crying because in a way, I felt culpable by association. This was the US—my country, my military—wreaking endless death and destruction on other human beings...Muslim human beings. My country was waging war on my culture.

When I was commissioned, I swore to protect and defend the United States of America. I was fiercely loyal to my country, but in my heart, I felt fear and anxiety for my Muslim brothers and sisters. I fingered my dog tags (they still said NRP–No Religious

Preference) and broke down in a fresh round of sobbing. I couldn't even begin to explain how I felt. Not to Phil and not to anyone else in the Army. I feared I would be suspected of treason if I displayed any ambivalence whatsoever toward this "campaign."

Despite Phil's repeated assurances that I was safe, I knew at some point my safety would no longer be in his hands—or mine. I began to weigh the likelihood that I might be sent into this war zone, a deployment that brought with it the possibility of being captured by enemy forces. My worst nightmare from basic training was now all too close to becoming a reality.

Even if that didn't happen, I needed to figure out how I was going to navigate my inner feelings and turmoil while carrying out my duties and responsibilities. The brevity of the war made that considerably easier. Even with the relentless bombardment of Iraqi and Kuwaiti targets, the 97th GH never received the high number of casualties we had prepared for, and for that, I was extremely grateful. Most of the patients we did get were for noncombat injuries.

It was a relief to all of us when we learned that a cease-fire was declared four days into the ground-operations phase of the war. Days later, as the cease-fire held and the details of a permanent end to hostilities were being worked out, we began to take our hospital off its war footing.

CHAPTER 16

BACK IN THE STATES

After three years in Europe, Phil and I departed for our next assignment. Although I had outranked him for much of the time, I happily pinned the golden oak leaf on his shoulder and we both left as majors.

We were posted to Fort Belvoir, Virginia and found a home in Mount Vernon on land that had once belonged to George Washington. By now, the childcare issues that threatened to overwhelm me earlier in my career were virtually nonexistent, since Hannah and Amal were quite independent.

Both Phil and I were assigned to DeWitt Army Community Hospital, an older, 46-bed facility that first opened in 1957. Phil worked in the operating room, and I stepped into an OB/GYN clinic mired in chaos: Open bickering among the physicians and chronic absenteeism. One obstetrician disappeared for long periods of time, ostensibly because she was "busy on the labor deck," leaving me and the other NP to see her scheduled patients in addition to our own. One day when I went to the labor-and-delivery deck to look for her, no one was there. I couldn't find anyone on staff who'd seen her that day at all. That was merely the tip of the iceberg.

Upon my arrival at DeWitt, I was assigned the role of acting head nurse—a huge burden in such a busy and dysfunctional environment—in addition to my primary assignment as women's healthcare NP. I was told not to worry because the head nurse job, a civilian position, would soon be filled by a permanent employee.

"Soon" turned out to be code for "never." Weeks later, I was informed that there was no head nurse position at DeWitt, neither military nor civilian. To procure one, a job description would have to be written, approved, and then passed up through the chain of command. In other words, I shouldn't hold my breath for a new head nurse. Meanwhile, I was supposed to keep doing both jobs at once. I was irate: I'd been sandbagged.

I created the necessary head nurse job description at home on my own time. Several weeks after I submitted it for approval, it landed back on my desk, apparently untouched. When I asked what happened, I was told it hadn't been forwarded because it was highly unlikely that it would be approved. I resubmitted it and pleaded with my superiors to look it over one more time and then pass it up to the next level.

The stress began to snowball as the clinic chief kept pushing more patients onto my calendar, leaving me less time to attend to my administrative duties, which also seemed to multiply. In addition to seeing scheduled patients, I attended monthly peer-review meetings and conducted weekly evening labor-and-delivery classes as NP. As head nurse, I conducted weekly new OB intake classes and participated in counseling and evaluation sessions for my subordinates. All of this came with mountains of paperwork. I had no alternative but to stay in the clinic after hours or bring the piles home with me, much like during my time at Fort Meade years earlier.

As head nurse, I also had to deal with the rampant underperformance in our clinic. While DeWitt's nursing staff was a mix of military and civilian personnel, the civilians were the most problematic, particularly several nursing assistants who would antagonize me and Staff Sergeant (SSG) Alvarez, my noncommissioned officer in charge (NCOIC). They flatly refused to carry out instructions from either of us, claiming, "It's not my job" or, "Why should I if I'm not appreciated?" They took frequent smoking breaks, left the clinic in the middle of the day without informing anyone, arrived late or departed early, and called in sick on snow days, even though they were considered essential staff. On several occasions, I found them socializing in an empty office as patients crowded our waiting room.

I initially tried positive reinforcement to solve the problem, praising them when I saw them doing something right, but it didn't help. In a more vigorous attempt to put an end to this discordant and, at times, belligerent behavior and to get these employees to understand what we expected of them, SSG Alvarez and I initiated a series of counseling sessions. Despite our efforts, there was no improvement. They knew perfectly well what was expected of them; they simply didn't want to do their jobs. Worse yet, as seasoned DOD civilian hires, they were experts at gaming the system. They knew precisely how many write-ups they could incur before being fired, and they were willing to exhaust this quota, stopping at the brink of termination.

I could only assume that my predecessors had let this egregious behavior slide for a long time. I couldn't do that; it wasn't in my nature as a person and was definitely unacceptable in the Army. Not only were these employees insubordinate but they had an adverse effect on our patients and clinic. To ignore their negative behavior would be disrespectful to the handful of dedicated, hard-working, and competent staff members in our clinic. And since fixing problems was part of my job and as head nurse I was responsible for the clinic as a whole and the actions of my staff, I wrote up the troublemakers.

Nevertheless, the theatrics continued. One incident in particular has stayed with me all these years. It happened when an angry patient cursed at one of the nursing assistants. She responded with a booming "fuck you" that reverberated across our waiting room. SSG Alvarez and I immediately summoned her to my office.

She slouched in a chair directly across from me, arms folded across her chest, and refused to make eye contact. Instead her eyes flitted around the room, as if she were the aggrieved party and had better things to do with her time. We asked her questions but she remained hostile and silent—not a word.

A week later, I received a letter from the Equal Employment Opportunity Commission (EEOC). This employee had accused me of racial discrimination. I gritted my teeth.

Was she really asking the EEOC to endorse the concept that yelling "fuck you" at a patient was somehow commonplace and acceptable in her culture and that I was at fault for not knowing that?

In alleging that I didn't understand her culture and language, one sentence was particularly galling, "While Major Johnson can speak perfect English, she doesn't understand it because she's not a born American." When I responded to the letter, I added that I interpreted her disparaging remarks about my English skills and about my being a naturalized citizen as a display of her own bias toward me.

The complaint was quickly dropped.

* * * * *

I already knew that enthusiasm was contagious. When I was posted to Fort McClellan in Alabama, the entire clinic was eager to do not just a good job but the best job possible. We were happy to support our colleagues through shared knowledge and expertise. It was the same at the 97th in Frankfurt, and then some. We were busy, but I looked forward to reporting for work each day.

But I learned at DeWitt that apathy and impudence are also contagious. The insolence of the entrenched civilian staffers spread quickly to new arrivals. One new nursing assistant, a young woman who was an active duty private first class, initially seemed to be doing her best work and was eager to improve. She displayed a reserved, yet positive, attitude and was respectful to everyone. However, within a few weeks, her conduct began to mirror the behavior of her problematic coworkers.

SSG Alvarez counseled her numerous times but she didn't respond. After repeated incidents of arrogant and rebellious behavior, I called her into my office. It was time for a reality check. In a firm but quiet manner, I informed her yet again that her conduct was unacceptable and then I pointed out the obvious. Unlike her surly civilian counterparts, she was in the Army.

This meant that unlike her pals, she was subject to the Uniform Code of Military Justice (UCMJ). I informed her that if she continued to be insubordinate, I was fully prepared to report her to the company commander for an Article 15, punishable by anything ranging from restrictions and extra duty to forfeiture of pay and reduction in rank. I never liked to lead by threat but it seemed warranted and it had the desired effect—I soon saw a remarkable improvement in her demeanor.

I presented these and other incidents up through my chain of command. The only response was to bring in a psychiatrist to hold weekly meetings with the entire clinic staff. These meetings soon devolved into little more than gripe fests. The air was never cleared, and the sessions actually created more problems than they solved. And because attendance was mandatory, the clinic was closed during the meetings. Incoming telephone calls went straight to voicemail, including some from panic-stricken women in labor. In the end, we made a lot of patients angry and got nothing for it.

I persisted in trying to solve our problems, meeting with each of my superior officers individually, but my words fell on deaf ears. They repeatedly gave the same response: "document and report."

For months, I did exactly that with no interventions or results.

Soon enough, my superiors began to treat me with indifference or hostility when I brought these issues to their attention.

I became a pariah in the clinic and was soon given a powerful reminder of how deeply my colleagues disliked me. On one particular day, I was booked solid with patients, many of whom were senior officers or wives of high-ranking officials. Most of them were coming in for their annual wellness exams, which included cervical cancer screenings.

Following strict protocol, I handled the specimens and sent them to the lab. But they were all returned to me a few days later, each with the same problem: "Unable to read due to inadequate preservative." I immediately called the lab, and the cytologist informed me that it appeared that the slides from my patients had been placed in water instead of the usual fixative.

All of them. And only mine.

None of the other tests done that day were affected. With a sick feeling in my stomach, I knew this was a deliberate act of sabotage by one of my staff members. Indeed, they had succeeded in making me look bad. I called each patient I'd seen that day, apologizing profusely, and asking her to return to the clinic to repeat the test.

But that wasn't the end of the retribution. While at DeWitt, I was passed over for promotion to lieutenant colonel for a second time. It was a humiliating experience. I'd worked extremely hard over the years, completed the required military and civilian education along the way, and maxed the physical fitness tests many times over. What more was I supposed to do?

I couldn't help but compare myself to those whose names *were* on the list—and I knew I was at least as qualified as those who'd been promoted.

Was I the victim of favoritism? Had I made myself too "difficult" by repeatedly raising issues of staff attitude and incompetence? Would I have made lieutenant colonel if I'd ignored the problems right before my eyes?

It was impossible for me to think otherwise. Throughout all this, my dear Phil remained my strongest champion and my best friend. His abundance of positive, loving words gave me so much needed support and encouragement. I also tried to draw on some of my father's favorite advice: "Always be grateful for everything, and focus on what you have, not on what you don't have."

With my father's gentle voice ringing in my ears, I readjusted my thinking. How could I not be grateful that I was an NP and a major in the US Army, instead of a woman in Saudi Arabia with a third-grade education? That's who I could've become had my father not made that critical decision back in 1960.

But with gratitude came responsibility. Something was seriously wrong at DeWitt, and clearly, I was the only one who could or *would* do anything about it. Besides, I was at the end of my tether. I was being penalized, sabotaged, and marked as a villain, both personally and professionally, just for doing my job and insisting that others do theirs.

My father's words again came to mind. Good Muslims, he would tell me, are not only judged by their own actions but also by how they respond to the actions of others. "If you witness a wrong and don't intervene to change it," he told me, paraphrasing from the *Book of Hadiths*, "You're just as responsible for that wrong action as the perpetrators themselves."

WHEN YOU WITNESS A WRONG

I finally realized that the culture of dysfunction at DeWitt was so entrenched throughout the chain of command that it was going to take someone from the outside to change it. I filed a multi-page complaint with the Inspector General (IG). As I enumerated the issues, I included supporting documentation for each item. Despite my grave concern about the possibility of retaliation, I concluded my report with a request that the IG's office launch an investigation.

I worried that things could get a lot worse because all of the officers I named in my complaint still had power over me. Even though the IG assured me that the Whistleblower Protection Act of 1989 would provide me with legal protection against any type of threat to my career, I was still taking a risk and I knew it.

The situation was serious enough to warrant a meeting with the chief and the assistant chief of the Army Nurse Corps. Both of them knew me personally from past assignments. Colonel Nancy Adams, who had been my chief nurse at the 97th GH in Frankfurt, had risen to become brigadier general and chief of the entire ANC. Colonel Terris Kennedy, the assistant chief of the ANC, had known me through previous assignments, conferences, and seminars I presented in.

In the meeting, I handed each of them a copy of my IG grievance report and asked them what I should do next. They encouraged me to do the hardest thing of all—sit tight and let the system do what it had been designed to do—to allow for due process. They assured me that the IG would conduct a thorough investigation and would come up with a set of recommended steps to address the problems I'd identified. Both women also gave me their full support. *Alhamdulillah!* I said to myself as I left their office.

Within a few days, staff from the IG's office were all over De-Witt interviewing every person I had named in my report as well as several other clinic and hospital personnel. I took extra care to watch my back—I was sure some of the people involved knew I was the one who'd brought in the IG but no one ever confronted me about it. About a month later, I received a copy of their report. They had looked into every issue I had put before them.

Shortly thereafter, the Army cleaned house. All the active-duty culprits I'd named were either reassigned or retired. Although this wholesale change was never officially presented as "cause and effect," the timing of what happened left little doubt that the Army was acting on the findings of the IG.

At about the same time, the head nurse position was approved and filled immediately. She took over all the administrative duties that had fallen to me. It became her responsibility to deal with our sullen, insubordinate nursing assistants. On the one hand, I knew this would be an unpleasant, ongoing challenge for her—it is still almost impossible to terminate even the worst DOD civilian personnel. On the other hand, I was relieved that this was not my problem anymore. I could go back to my role as an NP. I was also free once again to have a personal life—I no longer had to take endless reams of paperwork home with me. Those two reasons alone motivated me to persevere in reaching my goals. I also realized that persisting in my determination to be treated as an equal had paid off with good results for me.

I finally had more time to spend with my family, at least more time to spend with Hannah and Amal: Phil had been ordered to Somalia as part of a United Nations peacekeeping mission following years of famine and civil unrest.

He had only a couple of days to get ready. Since this was a mercy mission, I wasn't too worried about his deployment, at least not right away. It was a couple of weeks before I heard from him by phone, and he told me that conditions in Mogadishu, Somalia's capital, were considerably more dangerous than anyone had been led to expect. They'd set up their hospital on the playing field of an abandoned sports stadium at what had once been a university. Their living quarters were also on the field, only a few steps away. This was the entirety of their world—they were completely isolated from the rest of the city. Army personnel were safe within the confines of the stadium, but anarchy and lawlessness reigned just beyond the perimeter. Phil and the others could move freely inside the compound, but no one was permitted to leave.

It soon became clear how essential this precaution was. On October 3, 1993, forces loyal to a Somali warlord shot down two American Black Hawk helicopters and some of our troops were captured. Gruesome footage of US soldiers being dragged through the streets of Mogadishu aired repeatedly on newscasts in the States.

I fought off panic daily. Since the American camp was entirely fenced in, it seemed only logical that helicopters were being used to ferry people in and out. It was entirely possible that Phil could have been on one of those choppers during his recent rotation out of the country for R&R.

I asked my commander if he had any more information, but he knew nothing more than I did. The following week was agonizing until I finally heard from Phil. He was exhausted but okay. No one from his unit had been on the helicopters that were brought down, but they had to deal with the grisly human toll that followed the downing. Everyone in the stadium had been working up to 20 hours a day, treating a rush of patients with severe injuries. They were able to save some but not all. Many of the survivors would never be the same.

* * * * *

Phil came home right before Christmas of 1993. The girls and I were so happy to have him back and out of harm's way. One of his first jobs when he returned was to attend to my left shoulder. It wasn't injured—but I needed him to pin a silver oak leaf on it. I was finally a lieutenant colonel (LTC). I was relieved, grateful, and surprised. Being passed over as I had been, especially twice, often meant that chances for further promotion were remote. But when the next promotion board met, my name was at the top of the list. Becoming an LTC made me both joyous and proud, especially since the promotion had seemed like such an insurmountable obstacle when the situation at DeWitt was at its most toxic. Nevertheless, I kept doing my best in trying to succeed, and I knew that my perseverance would have made my father proud as well.

The pinning ceremony took place in mid-January 1994. Phil pinned my left shoulder. General Adams, chief nurse of the ANC, pinned my right.

Afterward, I hosted a celebration. I invited General Adams and Colonel Kennedy, as well as all my coworkers at DeWitt and friends stationed in other nearby facilities. For refreshments, I offered an array of Middle Eastern specialty foods and cake, all of which I made myself.

In 1995, when the active fighting ended at the end of the war in Bosnia, the US Army began treating thousands of refugee survivors, including many Muslim women who had been subjected to repeated sexual assault. I expressed my interest in this deployment as it seemed an excellent opportunity to use my particular expertise to help other Muslim women. I was initially chosen for that mission. However, the night before I was to deploy, another army nurse replaced me as part of a supposed political strategy. Needless to say, I was very disappointed, but I accepted it and moved on. I was hoping this wouldn't be my only chance to work with Muslim women.

Even though the IG investigation resulted in positive change at DeWitt, it still seemed like it was time to leave the clinic. Soon after I was promoted, I was selected for a newly created position as DeWitt's utilization management officer. The military healthcare system, like the civilian sector, was undergoing major changes. We were all learning how to provide more cost-effective care to our patients. Learning the job would mean taking on a new skill set, but its primary attraction was that it would free me from the clinic environment that had caused me so much mental and physical anguish.

At about the same time, the commander at the Naval Medical Clinic at Quantico Marine Base requested that a healthcare provider be sent to Quantico two and a half days a week to see their OB/GYN patients. My new superiors offered me this assignment if I could present a well- executed proposal of how I would balance it with my duties at DeWitt. I considered my vision of what I wanted my future in the ANC to be and happily accepted the offer; I then began to write my proposal.

Although I was still posted to Fort Belvoir, each of these new positions was considered a change of assignment. This meant that we could stay in one place while the girls were in high school. The tradeoff was that Phil and I were each posted overseas separately and on different assignments.

In 1995, Phil was sent to South Korea, and I was a single parent for a year. While Phil was gone, Hannah graduated from high school and started college. When he returned home, he was assigned to WRAMC until he retired. Then it was my turn.

CHAPTER 17

SOUTH KOREA

Four years later in April 1999, I was to report to my new assignment: South Korea. When Phil was posted there in 1995, he spent his tour at the 121st General Hospital in Seoul as part of the Yongsan Garrison, headquarters for US forces in South Korea. The amenities of Seoul, a modern Asian city, were just blocks away. In his words, his year was relatively "low stress." On the other hand, my experience was very different. I was assigned to Camp Casey near the town of Dongducheon.

It didn't take long to see why this deployment was considered hardship duty. Camp Casey is located only 11 miles below the Demilitarized Zone (DMZ), the no-man's land that marks the boundary between North and South Korea. (By contrast, Seoul is still 35 miles away). Active fighting in the Korean War had ceased in 1953 but because the two Koreas never declared a formal end to the conflict, the camp was on a permanent readiness footing. If North Korea invaded the South, American soldiers at Camp Casey would be the first and last best hope of stopping them before they reached Seoul.

I tried to learn as much as I could about Korean culture. I developed a liking for kimchi, the pungent national side dish that's served with almost everything. Made of fermented cabbage and spiced with garlic, onion, and hot pepper, the aroma wafted from every doorway. When I ate it, I could imagine it flowing from my own pores, such was its potency.

To protect the South Korean capital, the Army put the "best of the best" at Camp Casey. The post was home to several of the main combat units of the Second Infantry Division (2nd ID), and as a fighting force, they were "Second to None," which was actually their motto.

As the boxer Muhammed Ali once said, "It's not bragging if you can back it up." The 2nd ID was the most forward-deployed, lethal, and combat-ready division in the Army. In addition to artillery and engineering commands, units included armor, mechanized infantry, air assault infantry, and combat aviation. The best troops get the best weaponry and firepower and Camp Casey got it in abundance: Bradley fighting vehicles, Abrams tanks, Apache helicopters, and artillery with multiple launch rocket systems, to name a few.

The fact that our best troops were equipped with state-of-the-art weapons stood in stark contrast to the buildings they lived and worked in. They had never been state-of-the-art, even when they were new, which was before I was born. The structures at Camp Casey were relics left over from the Korean War, if not from World War II. They reminded me of East Germany.

If the Troop Medical Clinic where I would be working was antiquated, the senior officers' quarters were borderline primitive. My home-away-from-home was a bare-bones studio apartment—a bedroom with a bathroom, period. It had been outfitted with basic Army-issue furniture, refrigerator, and window air conditioner. I shared a kitchen and laundry room with seven other officers.

Being a Woman in a "Second to None" Male Environment

At our clinic, the medical staff included the clinic chief and head nurse, both majors; several MDs, all captains; the clinic NCO-IC, who was a staff sergeant; and medics ranging from private to specialist. Then there was me, the lieutenant colonel. I outranked not only everyone else in the clinic but everyone else in the camp.

As a women's healthcare NP, I provided sexually transmitted disease counseling, diagnosis, and treatment, along with regular gynecological exams, contraception, and pregnancy testing. Sadly, but not surprisingly, I also treated young active duty women who had been the victims of sexual assault by their fellow soldiers and officers. Each time I did so, old memories of Nadir's abuse—verbal, physical, and sexual—came flooding back, shaking me to the core.

Being the highest-ranking officer at Camp Casey certainly had its benefits, but I was always careful not to abuse my position. To the contrary, I felt it was incumbent upon me to set an example and serve as a role model for both officers and enlisted personnel, whether I was on duty or on my own time. And it seemed to me that there was a dire shortage of positive role models in the leadership of the second infantry, particularly when it came to how our women soldiers were treated.

At the 2nd ID, a whole lot of male ego was tied up in being "Second to None," which often revealed itself in really ugly sexist conduct. Senior officers and NCOs might have deluded themselves thinking that "boys will be boys" but this went way beyond locker room talk or frat-house humor. Many women, myself included, found the chauvinistic male environment to be both overwhelming and threatening. Not surprisingly, the youngest enlisted women got the worst of it. Crude, in-your-face, macho behaviors were common enough to be considered "normal." There were highly sexualized catcalls, gestures, and innuendos, as well as groping and other unwanted physical advances. On a day-to-day basis, many women at Camp Casey felt like prey. They worried less about an attack by the North Koreans than they did about a personal assault by their fellow soldiers.

I was spared most of it because I was a senior officer, but I saw plenty of incidents in which noncoms and junior officers harassed or demeaned female soldiers. One such incident occurred during normal duty hours. A young female soldier was brought into the clinic with a fractured leg. I was busy with my scheduled patients and couldn't help but hear the agonizing screams piercing from the exam room next door. The guttural crying sounded ominous to me and continued even after she received pain medication. After finishing with my patients, I went to comfort her.

"Are you still in pain?" I asked the attractive young blonde lying on the exam table.

"Yes," she replied, bursting out in tears.

"Is the pain medication not effective?" Her deep reaction seemed inappropriate. I had a hunch something bigger was hurting her. Something other than her fractured leg. I sat with her for close to two hours during which time she received another dose of pain medication. But she was still crying. When she finally shared with me what had happened, I was shocked. As it turned out, she fractured her leg because she was trying to hide from her abuser, a sergeant who preyed on young enlisted women. He was knocking on the door to her barracks and was about to enter. She tried to hide from him by going out of her second-floor window and hanging onto the windowsill. She broke her leg when she fell.

It didn't take me very long to report this sergeant to his company commander. In the end, I learned that she was reassigned stateside and he remained at Camp Casey. This was how these incidents usually resulted.

Women were vulnerable even off duty. The worst behavior was alcohol-fueled. Soju, the national booze of Korea, is a potent, clear, distilled liquor. Bars catering to GIs often served it mixed with sweetened fruit juice or Kool-Aid. The resulting sugary beverage was known as a kettle, and it was the drink of choice for the 2nd ID. Thirsty soldiers downed them as if they were beers but they were a lot stronger than your average Budweiser. With each round of kettles, the troops got louder and rowdier, and many of them kept drinking until they got sloshed. Women who went out drinking with their buddies ended up having to fend them off before the night was over. It was all too reminiscent of what happened at the regimental mess at Fort McClellan when I was a young captain.

The clinic doctors were all men, except for Captain Thuy Tran, whose family had come from Vietnam. The NCOIC, Sergeant Sophie Miller, was also an Asian-American from Thailand. As a matter of policy, the Army discourages fraternization between officers and enlisted personnel but since all of us worked closely together, Thuy and I included Sophie in our outings and became friends. My friendship with these remarkable women was the most satisfying part of my year in Korea.

Thuy, Sophie, and I were walking around town on a Saturday afternoon when we passed two young soldiers. One of them called out "Ching, Chong Chinaman!" while the other giggled. I did a 180, stopped them, and asked them how it would feel if they heard a racial slur meant against them. They were speechless. After I identified myself and my rank, they apologized. I wanted them to feel compassion. Whether or not they did, I'll never know.

Whenever possible, I tried to intervene, using my rank to turn these negative incidents into a teaching moment for the perpetrators. This was something I'd first learned from my father as a girl in Cairo—that in every life experience, there is always an opportunity for teaching and/or for learning.

In the wee hours of a summer morning, I was awakened from a sound sleep by a phone call. It was Thuy, who was the doctor on duty at the clinic's emergency room. She needed my assistance with a young female soldier who had come into the ER around midnight complaining of abdominal cramping and nausea without an elevated temperature.

Thuy called me rather than her physician colleagues because she feared they would belittle her for asking for help. She was the only woman MD, and in the testosterone-saturated environment of Camp Casey, she had already endured more than enough of their slights and taunts about her competence as a doctor.

When Thuy met me at the entrance, I could hear her patient groaning and crying out in the exam room.

Her name was Kayla Wilson, and as I introduced myself to her, I could see that she was extremely fit—as were all the soldiers in the second infantry.

"How long have you been feeling this way?" I asked.

"Since last night, ma'am," she told me. "I'd just completed a 12-mile hike with full pack and I was starving. I grabbed the first thing I saw in the fridge, a turkey sandwich."

"How long had it been in there?" Dr. Tran asked.

"I don't know," Kayla replied. "At that moment, I was so hungry I didn't really care. Guess I gave myself a case of food poisoning."

"Not necessarily," I said. "Let's have a look."

As I was examining Kayla, I asked when her last menstrual period was. She didn't remember. Her cycle had been irregular, she said, ever since she was posted to Camp Casey. She chalked it up to the extensive physical training required of the soldiers. Then she mentioned that she had cramping pain primarily along the lower left abdomen.

For me, that was a meaningful clue. I immediately began conducting a gynecological exam and got quite a surprise. Her cervix was eight to nine centimeters dilated, and there was a fetal head presenting at the opening.

"You're pregnant, Kayla," I told her.

"No way!" she said, astonished.

"Way," I replied. "And you're at term and having contractions. That's why you've been experiencing cramps and nausea. You're in labor. That turkey sandwich is innocent. It had nothing to do with how you're feeling."

It was inevitable that she was going to deliver soon. As Thuy and a medic began prepping the room for delivery, I left to call the obstetrician at the 121st General Hospital in Yongsan. After I explained the situation, he recommended that we air-evac our patient to him immediately. I was skeptical—I didn't think we had that much time. Nevertheless, I asked the medic to call for the chopper.

Meanwhile, in between moans of pain, Kayla was still trying to come to terms with her condition. "But how can this be? I didn't gain any weight. I just completed the 12-mile march!" she exclaimed.

Kayla deserved a fitness medal—that march was grueling for any soldier, let alone one in the ninth month of pregnancy. Troops had to cover the 12-mile course in three hours or less and they were outfitted in full gear: Pistol belt with suspenders and two full ammunition pouches, two water-filled canteens, first aid pack, poncho, Kevlar helmet, M-16 rifle with six magazines, protective mask with carrier, bayonet, and a 35-pound rucksack. Successful completion was more than a badge of honor—it was also a prerequisite for individual advancement to specialized higher training, as well as for Air Assault School.

From her physical appearance, no one would have thought Kayla was pregnant. Her abdomen was taut and firm and didn't have the distended basketball or watermelon shape we would expect to see. Even so, I thought, Kayla herself must have had some inkling based on fetal movement or difficulty sleeping, or even indigestion. "You didn't feel anything different these last few months," I asked. "Excessive tiredness, nausea, or kicking in your belly?"

"I thought maybe I had gas, or that my stomach was grumbling," she replied. "I didn't make a big deal of it. Sure, I was tired, but I figured it was all because I was training so hard for that march."

"I know this is a lot to process, Kayla, but it's too late to send you to the 121st," I said softly. "It's too risky, both for you and for your child. As far as the baby is concerned, it's go time. What I need you to do now is push with each cramp, okay?"

As Kayla was pushing, Thuy and I coached her to breathe slowly and deeply between contractions and to push only when she felt one. By now it was 7:00 a.m., time for shift change. As soon as Thuy's replacement arrived, he immediately tried to assert control.

"I'll take it from here!" he announced, far too eagerly.

He was already gloved and brandishing a scalpel. He hadn't even bothered to introduce himself to the patient—to her face—but had somehow assumed he was going to immediately perform an episiotomy on her perineum. How rude! How disrespectful! It had been awhile since I'd seen such boundless conceit and lack of professionalism.

Thuy sighed and rolled her eyes. No wonder she'd called me in the middle of the night instead of this insensitive, self-important colleague. Maybe Dr. Arrogant thought he could elbow Thuy, his fellow captain, out of the way, but he wasn't going to get away with that with me. I'd been an RN for 25 years and a women's healthcare NP for 15 of those years—it's not as if I needed a smug, inexperienced MD to tell me how to assist a woman in the final stages of labor. If ever there was a teaching moment, this was it.

"We don't need an episiotomy, *Captain*. All the situation requires is a few more pushes," l said without looking at him. My full focus and attention were on my patient and the newborn head that was about to emerge.

"My shift has started, and I'm in charge of the emergency room now," Dr. Arrogant insisted.

I ignored him as I continued coaching Kayla. With another push, I eased the baby's head through the stretched perineum. With the next, I guided the shoulders. After that, the baby slipped into the world with ease. No tear. No episiotomy.

"It's a girl!" I announced. "A big, beautiful baby girl!"

Joy registered immediately in Kayla's eyes. I was happy for her, and I was especially happy that we had been able to prevent an unnecessary episiotomy. As Dr. Arrogant sulked in a corner, the placenta was delivered shortly thereafter.

I accompanied Kayla and her newborn on the chopper to Yongsan. The baby appeared normal and healthy. Strictly speaking, the medevac helicopter wasn't necessary but it still had to return to Seoul either with or without us.

Dr. Arrogant's ego was sufficiently bruised, so much so that he reported me to the clinic chief. I was not surprised that nothing came of his complaint, but it was yet another manifestation of testosterone overload at Camp Casey.

Two weeks later, Kayla came by the clinic to thank Thuy and me for our help. She also came to say goodbye. She was about to be reassigned out of South Korea, but in the meantime, she wanted us to know that she'd chosen a name for her daughter: Casey.

CHAPTER 18

WALTER REED, AGAIN

In my last years in the Army, I was assigned to WRAMC two more times, and those postings bookended my time in South Korea.

On my first return to Walter Reed in October 1997, I was assigned as the head nurse on Ward 68. Upon my arrival to the unit, I found myself reminiscing about my first posting at WRAMC. I was newly out of basic training and assigned to Ward 67, which primarily treated women with cancer. I loved my job, even though I got written up when my babysitters didn't show and I had to park Hannah and Amal in the nurses' station while I worked my shift. I recalled the times when I had no other choice but to have Hannah and Amal in tow when I reported for night shift duty. Taking the girls out of their beds and bringing them to the hospital with me, setting up their little lairs in the nurses' station where they slept all night while I worked. They were oh-so-cute and never complained about it. Neither did my coworkers. My head nurse was the only one who wrote me up.

Now the girls were in their twenties, and I was in charge of Ward 68, the largest, most demanding unit in the Army's flagship medical center; I was indeed back in the same place but a long way from where I'd started.

I oversaw a staff of 13 nurses, some military, ranging in rank from second lieutenant to major, and some civilian. I also indirectly supervised the rest of the staff, making sure that a standard of excellence was maintained. Ward 68 was an extremely busy surgical ward with preoperative and postoperative general-surgery patients, plus transfers from the intensive care step-down unit. We also took care of challenging orthopedic, neurosurgery, and reconstructive surgery cases, some of which had been referred to us from overseas hospitals and combat zones. With this caseload, foot traffic on the ward was intense. In addition to our own nursing staff, we had a continuous stream of surgeons, residents, medical and nursing students, x-ray technologists, phlebotomists, dieticians, and physical therapists. In short, we bustled.

On Ward 68, surgical residents made daily rounds with their superiors, all seasoned surgeons. They went from room to room examining patients, then stepped into the corridor to discuss their observations about each patient's condition. The surgeons grilled the residents about specific issues and treatment plans. Either my assistant head nurse or I stayed with the group, taking notes on anything in the discussion that pertained to nursing care in order to facilitate communication and respond quickly to patient and physician concerns and next steps in treatment.

The ward ran smoothly most of the time, thanks to a great team of healthcare providers and support staff. Outliers and aberrations did occur, however, and when they did, the individuals involved made every effort to resolve the issue quickly and efficiently at their own level before it reached the ward master, the assistant head nurse, or me. I rarely needed to directly intervene, and if I did, it was either for the well-being of our patients or to defend my staff.

I was a real tiger about both of those issues because I saw them as interrelated. My priority was making sure that our patients, many of whom were recuperating after complex surgeries, received the best possible care. That could only happen if nurses were incentivized to provide it and were treated like the dedicated professionals they are. Just as field officers are responsible for the troops under their command, I was responsible for my staff, including their morale. I knew that if I demanded excellence from my team while showing them that I had their back, they would knock themselves out to do the best they could for me. As part of my job, I actively participated in what happened on my ward. When necessary, I got my hands dirty, working alongside my nurses to do the very physical work of providing patient care.

In our busy environment, courtesy, mutual respect, open communication, and teamwork were vital. Most of the doctors were professional, friendly, and respectful to me and my staff with one notable exception: Dr. Matthew McDermott. He was a captain and a cocky first-year orthopedic resident who was repeatedly dismissive and downright rude to my nurses. Several lieutenants and enlisted staff members reported his behavior to me.

Simply put, he treated them like "the help," as if they were maids and servants. In his opinion, their job was to instantly obey his every command and he unabashedly yelled at them if they didn't respond fast enough. He threw soiled tape and dressings onto the floor rather than into the trash with the expectation that they would clean up after him. When one of the RNs, a lieutenant, tried to speak with him about it, he shouted, "That's *your* job, not mine!"

Things came to a head when he removed an intravenous needle from a patient's arm and walked away, leaving the unsanitary dressing and tubing—and the needle—next to the patient. He'd left a sharp and a potential biohazard in the bed, creating an unsafe condition for both the patient and the staff. When one of my nurses called him out on it, he began yelling—again—about how he was the doctor and we all had to defer to him about everything.

I knew I had to do something. Even though Captain McDermott was not in my chain of command, his unprofessional demeanor was affecting the morale of my people. I entered the room, snapped on a pair of latex gloves, and disposed of the dressing, tubing, and needle. Then I told Dr. McDermott to get out of the unit.

He refused. "I'm the doctor," he bellowed. He continued shouting, this time at me, and his nonstop harangue started to attract a crowd. Patients, staff, and visitors passing in the corridor now clogged the doorway, gawking at the spectacle.

"You can't ask me to leave!" he yelled finally, believing he had the last word.

"Actually, I can," I replied calmly, standing my ground. I deliberately kept my voice down. "I'm not asking you to leave, Captain McDermott. I'm *telling* you to leave."

"You can't do that!" he screamed.

"This is not a suggestion. I'm giving you a *direct order, Captain.* I'm commanding you to remove yourself from this ward—*STAT.*"

He was a doctor. I was a nurse. He was a captain. I was a lieutenant colonel. We faced off in silence for a few seconds, and I could almost see the wheels churning as he ran through various alternative scenarios in his mind. I could also imagine them grinding to a halt when he figured it out.

This was the Army and he was in it. And this was an Army hospital, which meant that my silver oak leaf would prevail over his silver bars. As he sauntered his way past the gawkers and into the hall, I called after him that he could return once he'd cooled off but not until he modified his behavior. Several nurses who had witnessed the confrontation looked at me with relief and appreciation.

Later that afternoon, I attended a regularly scheduled multidisciplinary meeting of head nurses, section supervisors, senior surgeons, and other Walter Reed department heads. At the meeting, I brought up my morning showdown with Captain McDermott, as well as his prior run-ins with my nurses. I didn't mention him by name but I did identify him as a first-year orthopedic resident, and I made it very clear that his behavior was not only petulant and immature but was unbecoming conduct that wouldn't be tolerated on my unit.

The next day, I was summoned to my chief nurse's office. Colonel Jeri Graham was a full colonel, and she told me she'd received a visit from the chief of surgery, who was also a full colonel. Captain McDermott had complained bitterly to him, alleging that I had humiliated him in front of staff. I explained to her what happened.

The chief of surgery had been present in the meeting the prior day, and although he said nothing after I spoke, he had issues with what I'd said and done. He thought I shouldn't have challenged Dr. McDermott in front of an audience. He also thought it was wrong of me to bring up the incident in a meeting of peers instead of coming directly to him. And now he wanted Jeri Graham to do something about it. "He came into my office, and said, 'Speaking colonel to colonel, I'm asking you to reprimand her,'" Colonel Graham told me.

I'm sure my eyes registered alarm because she quickly shook her head and then broke into a smile. "'Speaking colonel to colonel,' I told him, 'I refuse. Your resident humiliated himself. Captain McDermott was way out of line. There's no way any nurse should have to put up with that crap even once, let alone repeatedly.'"

I breathed a sigh of relief as she added, "Frankly, I'm glad you put the kibosh on that one. You nipped it in the bud—this guy's behavior was only going to get worse."

I was happy to have a strong chief nurse who stood up for me and wasn't cowed by young surgeons and their tantrums. I also knew that if we were in a civilian hospital, I would have been in a lot of trouble. In a nonmilitary setting, there would have been no colonel-to-colonel conversation, and the "director of nursing" would have had to take direction from the "head of surgery." "Thank you so much for your support, ma'am," I told her.

It's clear to me now that being able to stand up for my nurses at Walter Reed and having the chief nurse stand up for me was excellent preparation for refusing to yield to a scalpel-happy young doctor in South Korea.

CHAPTER 19

WRAMC—THE FINAL TOUR

When I got back from Camp Casey, I was assigned to WRAMC for the third time. It would also be my last. After this assignment, I'd have completed 20 years of military service and would be eligible to retire.

The last assignment was something of a victory lap. I was to serve as the evening/night nursing supervisor, which in essence meant I was the stand-in for the hospital's chief nurse when she wasn't there. I embraced it for any number of reasons, above all because Phil and I didn't have to move and because I wasn't faced with a mountain of paperwork to take home. Beyond that, the position itself was satisfying and I truly enjoyed the camaraderie of the other evening/night nursing supervisors who shared the rotations with me. As I made rounds to all units at least twice per shift, I was able to interact with nurses and physicians in every department of Walter Reed.

My favorite unit was Ward 72. This was the VIP unit—only generals and high-ranking civilian dignitaries were admitted there. I felt honored to meet some of them, including Senators Strom Thurmond and Bob Dole and Supreme Court Justice Sandra Day

O'Connor. I was most impressed by Justice O'Connor, who made me feel very comfortable talking to her, as if she were like any other patient.

Whenever I arrived at a unit, I verified that all staff members were present. Then I checked on the status of patients in general and especially those who were of particular concern to the hospital commander and the chief nurse. As had been the case when I was in charge of Ward 68, I didn't hesitate to help if the situation required it. And I did so for the same two reasons: to ensure excellent patient care and defend the nurses who provided it.

One evening, I checked into a ward and saw young nurses, all lieutenants, dashing through the corridors at top speed as they tried to keep up with the needs of their patients. The ward was obviously shorthanded, but when I asked the RNs where the medics were, none of them knew, or at least that's what they told me. I pitched in to alleviate the immediate crisis, then I started looking for the missing medics.

I found them all right. One was sleeping in a vacant patient's room with the lights turned out and his boots off.

"Get up, soldier!" I commanded, turning on the lights. Startled, the young trooper jumped up immediately.

"Yes ma'am," he sheepishly replied as he rushed to put his boots on.

"I expect you to get back to your ward immediately," I told him as he was leaving the room.

I found two more in the patient activity room, laughing and joking.

"Now, explain to me what's so funny?" I asked without emotion or expression.

They cringed when I walked in on them. Apparently, my no-nonsense reputation had preceded me—as well it should have.

I was furious with the lot of them and demanded they got back to work, on the double.

"Yes ma'am," they replied in unison.

These muscular, burly guys had somehow intimidated the nurses on the ward into letting them get away with this behavior but I didn't have a problem confronting them about it. I also reported the problem to the chief nurse to ensure it didn't happen again, as per my duty.

CELEBRATING THE 100TH BIRTHDAY OF THE ARMY NURSE CORPS

Since being freed from double duty at Fort Belvoir (as head nurse and NP) and the chaos it created, I had more time to spend leisurely rather than taking work home each day. I had almost forgotten how liberating it felt to have the time and energy to do other things. I partook in family time, a social life, reading, and hobbies.

I had always loved to bake, which was a legacy from my grandmother. Some of my fondest childhood memories take place in her kitchen, listening to her explain what she was doing as she measured out each ingredient and "helping" as much as a young child could. To me, those times and the marvelous aromas emanating from the oven were always the essence of love and comfort. They still are today.

As much as I loved baking, I never knew how to make my baked goods look elegant. At about the time I relinquished my head nurse duties (at DeWitt), I signed up for a cake decorating course offered at our local craft store. By the time I perfected my skills, I'd become so busy that my kitchen was always hopping. I had myself a regular little bakery. Colleagues at DeWitt were soon asking me to bake cakes for them and now I was able to decorate them to order. I started baking custom cakes for birthdays, promotions, farewell parties, baby showers, christenings, and even weddings. Before long, I began receiving orders from other units at Fort Belvoir, WRAMC, and the Pentagon. People appreciated the artistry in my work, and in my own way, I could contribute to their celebrations of milestone events. It made them happy and it made me happy too, as I realized the launch of my new passion.

February 2, 2001, marked the 100th birthday of the ANC, and celebrations took place at Army medical posts across the country. Walter Reed hosted a huge luncheon, and as my reputation as a baker preceded the event, I was asked to bake and design a cake that was large enough for at least 75 servings.

The triple layer, 16-inch, yellow round cake was filled with raspberry and cream filling and iced with white whipped cream. I decorated the top with the words *Army Nurse Corps, 100 Years, 1901 – 2001* and the ANC caduceus, two snakes entwined around a winged staff, made of royal icing.

It made me feel good that everyone enjoyed it, and I was asked to make another just like it, except much bigger, for a dress-blue dinner event for over 200 people to celebrate the ANC centennial birthday in the greater DC area. As honored as I was to be entrusted with the project, it was also stressful. I *had* to get it right.

And I did. The second cake was three times larger than the first—it was so big that Phil and I had to take the rear seats out of our van to transport it. The enormous rectangular dessert was also very heavy. The two of us struggled as we lugged it from the kitchen—the last thing I wanted to do was drop it.

Phil liked to watch me bake because it gave me such joy. He, too, appreciated the art and mastery it required and cheered me on every time I completed a project. He encouraged me no matter how long it took to finish an order. And he delighted in sharing what he called the "cake scraps" with Hannah and Amal whenever they were home.

The cake occupied a place of honor in the reception area, flanked by photos and memorabilia of the history of the ANC. I was honored to hear guests comment on its perfect exquisiteness and how delicious it tasted. Although several individuals were lauded for planning, organizing, and otherwise contributing to both events, no one acknowledged the baker. There was no mention that an Army nurse had made the cake for the ANC centennial birthday celebrations. Little did anyone know that an *immigrant, Arab, Muslim Army nurse* had provided the cakes for both occasions. By the end of the evening, I felt like a musician who'd given a virtuoso performance to no applause.

But I remained cheerful, reminding myself that these feelings were only of my ego not having met my expectations. Once more, I thought about my father's immutable advice: "…Focus on what you have, not on what you don't have." I felt grateful for having been honored and trusted to accomplish this task in the first place. And with Phil's love, support, and encouragement, I was able to redirect my thoughts.

Is it really that bad? I asked myself. In the big picture, of course it wasn't. I thought about the many disappointments I had managed to live through and this was nothing, comparatively speaking.

I was determined to feel better and appreciated the strength to handle this situation as well.

PART IV

CHAPTER 20

COMING FULL CIRCLE

We shall not cease from exploration
And the end of all our exploring
Will be to arrive where we started
And know the place for the first time.

~ T.S. Eliot

"A re you watching TV?" I sensed a hint of panic in Amal's voice. She had skipped over her usual greeting and exchange of pleasantries. She was calling from the small federal government agency in downtown Washington, DC where she worked. Phil and I were having breakfast while watching the morning news. We sat there, stunned, as we watched the footage of two commercial airplanes crashing into the Twin Towers in New York City. Huge flames lapped from the buildings, and smoke billowed into the clear blue sky on what was otherwise a perfect early-fall morning. There was utter chaos on the ground as panicked people ran from the buildings.

"Yes, I'm watching. Are you okay?" I replied nervously.

"Yes" she said. "I'm okay." But the fear was obvious in her voice.

While we were talking about what the nation had just witnessed live on television, the news switched to another special report, indicating the Pentagon had also just been hit by a large passenger plane. More scenes of chaos and panic ensued as I watched the Pentagon burn. In disbelief, I thought back to the many times I had walked down the halls of that building throughout my career.

From where I stood in the kitchen of our sprawling home in South Bend, Indiana, the sky on September 11, 2001 was also beautiful, blue, and cloudless, and the changing colors of the leaves on the trees with the slight chill in the air told us fall was approaching. I had just arrived in South Bend only three days earlier on terminal leave while waiting my final retirement day from the Army. After 20 years of service, my official retirement date was set for October 1, 2001. I turned back to the TV in complete disbelief at what I saw. My immediate inclination was to call my unit at Walter Reed Army Medical Center in Washington DC and ask if I needed to return to DC. Phil suggested to wait and see if they called me.

"I don't know what to do," Amal continued. "They've told us we can all go home but none of the trains or buses can cross the bridges because they've all been closed. I think I'll have to walk."

I cautioned her to be careful. The six-mile walk home wouldn't be a problem for her, but still I worried. What mother wouldn't? Just as soon as I hung up with Amal, Hannah called, also in a panic.

"Mom? I don't know what's going on, but we heard on the news that two airplanes hit the Twin Towers in NYC, and now we hear a plane has crashed into the Pentagon." She lived in Alexandria and was also calling from her job in DC.

"Are you all right?" I asked her. I wished I were still living in Virginia so I could be with my girls.

"They told us to all go home, but there's no way I can drive home. The whole city is shut down and the cops are everywhere," Hannah said.

After I hung up the phone, I stared at the images of the Twin Towers on TV, burning like two cigarettes, and wondered how this could have happened. How could a group of people hate the United States so much that they would go to such extremes to destroy it? This was the country that gave my family the opportunity, peace, and security that most people in the world could only dream of. The alternating scenes between fear and sorrow on the ash-covered faces of New Yorkers running for safety and the celebrations in the Middle East, primarily among Palestinians, were mind boggling. While part of me was utterly appalled at seeing the Palestinians dancing in the streets, another part of me wondered if they were so happy because they themselves had experienced the horrors of ongoing terrorism for generations and probably wanted us to feel their pain.

Still, I stood there watching the footage, perplexed and unable to connect how one group of people could take such pleasure in another's pain and suffering. While I can't even attempt to explain or even theorize on the politics and events leading up to September 11, that fateful day impacted me as an American citizen, as a soon-to-be-retired US Army officer, and most of all, as an immigrant from Egypt.

I landed in New York City in 1960. Now 40 years later, watching the events of 9/11 unfold before me, I thought a lot about life coming around full circle, yet still leaving you a long way from where you started.

EPILOGUE

Your daily life is your temple and your religion. When you enter into it, take with you your all.

~ Khalil Gibran

When I retired, I realized I was probably the highest-ranking Arab immigrant Muslim woman to have served in the US Armed Forces. It's likely that I was also the first to wear the uniform, but we may never know for sure because Army recordkeeping doesn't accurately track this kind of data. As someone who doesn't believe in coincidences, it seemed more than serendipitous that I was born in Egypt on November 11, a day celebrated as Veteran's Day in the United States. At the time, it was impossible to imagine that this would be the country whose shores and citizens I would defend through military service three decades later.

As I mourned the loss of lives along with my fellow Americans and contemplated how the events of that fateful day would go on to impact the part of the world from which I came, Phil and I began a new chapter of our lives together in South Bend.

We'd sold our house in Virginia a few weeks earlier. The ability to serve my fellow human beings had been at the root of my decision to become a nurse, as well as my decision to join the Army. What I had come to understand over the course of my career is that there's always a way to help people if you look. I wasn't quite ready to end my nursing career, so I found several opportunities to continue helping people in my community by doing what I loved professionally. I worked as a nurse at the public schools nearby and at a few nonprofit organizations. In my free time, I tended to my garden and volunteered at a local agency that supports women and children. Our collective responsibility to serve others is something I learned from my father and by JFK's 1961 inaugural address.

One of the greatest lessons I hope my story can demonstrate is that there are good people of all cultures, nationalities, skin color, and religious faiths—and of no religious faith whatsoever. Not all Arabs are like Nadir and his family. Although they unfortunately fit a stereotype that too many Americans are eager to believe, the truth is that no culture is unchangeable or inflexible. In the Arab world, just as in the United States, Europe, Africa, Asia, and Latin America, there are people who victimize women and those who condone domestic violence. There are also increasing numbers of people who are staunch proponents of women's rights. In the Middle East, as elsewhere, views on domestic abuse are evolving.

In addition, I learned the hard way that Islam, like Judaism and Christianity, isn't monolithic. Although the basic tenets and pillars are the same, every culture and subculture has its own interpretation. The harsh Islamic "tradition" that Nadir and his parents believed in was radically different from my own, even though we both came from Egypt. My Muslim faith is that of my father's—and the spirit of this gentle, life-affirming man lives on not in Nadir but in Phil.

Phil is Catholic. He came into my life just six months after my father's passing, and I quickly learned that I could trust him with my deepest thoughts, feelings, and fears. He soon became my greatest advocate and my best friend, as well as a superlative father and role model for my daughters. Hannah and Amal were raised to be compassionate, honest, and loving to everyone they encountered, and this to me resonates much more deeply than adherence to any religious doctrine.

I hope my journey and the lessons I learned along the way can help forge a connection and greater understanding between Arab, Muslim, and American culture. Our diversity is the fabric of America. Even though tolerance is in woefully short supply in our world today, I pray that my story will help people realize this: Regardless of faith, nationality, skin color, ethnicity, or gender, we all have the same needs and the same desire for safety, acceptance, love, and happiness. That fundamental human truth can be the bridge to understanding and cooperation, the bridge that will connect us all.

While I hadn't actively looked for a mosque in our area, I was invited to attend an interfaith women's group meeting at the mosque in a neighboring town more than 10 years after I moved back to Indiana. I was pleasantly surprised to learn there was one there, and I welcomed the opportunity. I felt excited at the prospect of being able to share my experiences on a deeper level with others in my community with whom I might connect in a way that I couldn't with my other friends.

Growing up in America in the '60s and '70s, I had often felt alone and the "other." Back then, life became easier when we *hid* our cultural identity in order to gain acceptance into American society. After 50 years, however, things had changed drastically. With the growth of Islamic fundamentalism and the influx of millions of Muslims into the United States from around the world, I came to understand that my faith, although it is the same now as it was when I was a child, was perceived as "Americanized" and what I had to say about Islam was disregarded by many of the Muslim women. Attending the meeting at the mosque was uncomfortable for me and I didn't feel that I belonged there. It was a reminder that I was still the "other," which only further confirmed that I still don't fit into a single category. Searching for balance in my identity will continue to be a lifelong journey.

Years later, during the 2016 presidential election campaign, upon hearing then-candidate Donald Trump's disparaging remarks toward Muslims in general and in particular to the family of Army Captain Humayun Khan, who died in Iraq in service to this country, I felt compelled to speak up. I wrote a letter to President Barack Obama sharing my story as an Arab immigrant Muslim woman, retired from the US Army. I sent it off without thinking about it again and without telling anyone else about it. I certainly didn't expect a reply. Several months passed. Then on January 14, 2017, days before the inauguration of Donald Trump, I had a vivid dream that I was sitting in a garden, drinking tea, and visiting with President Obama. It was enchanting and seemed so real that when I woke up, I quickly tried to will myself back into the dream. It didn't work.

I began to weep. Phil, lying next to me, asked me what was wrong. When I told him about my dream, he smiled and tried to comfort me. A few days later, I told some friends about my dream. Then to my surprise, on January 20, 2017—Inauguration Day—I found an envelope in my mailbox with a return address: The White House. What I thought would be a dreadful day for me—watching in horror as a man I didn't believe was remotely fit to lead our country was sworn in as President—instead became one of the happiest days of my life. The envelope was postmarked January 17, 2017. I immediately opened it and saw that the letter itself was dated January 11, 2017. That's when I realized President Obama's reply to my letter had been on its way while I dreamt of visiting with him.

Coincidence or providence? Was this an answer to my deep-rooted desire to reach a president of the United States after hearing President Kennedy's captivating inauguration speech more than half a century ago?

Other than very little family memorabilia, my letter from President Barack Obama, which I've included as the final page of this memoir, is one of the most precious items I own, in large part because his warm, personal reply addressed my concerns. After a life spent trying to find and validate my place in this world, I felt honored to have the president of the most powerful nation in the free world hear me and understand me.

In the end, each of us has a story to tell and an inherent need to know that our stories matter…that *we* matter. Although no two stories can ever be entirely alike, we can find common ground in each other's experiences and the strength to move forward during difficult times.

I may never know what it feels like to check a box or easily fit into a category in order to feel equal, but I find comfort in knowing that my story, however tumultuous it may be, is my own. It may have the power to matter to someone else.

Even the president of the United States.

THE WHITE HOUSE
WASHINGTON

January 11, 2017

LTC Mona Johnson, USA (Ret)
South Bend, Indiana

Dear Colonel Johnson:

Thank you for sharing your story. Being American is about more than what we look like or how we worship. What makes us American is our commitment to the principles upon which our Union was founded: pluralism and openness, the rule of law, civil liberties, and the self-evident truth—expanded with each generation—that we are all created equal.

The United States of America was founded so that people could practice their faiths as they choose, and our Constitution is clear that we do not have religious tests. What separates us from tyrants and terrorists is that we have sacrificed and struggled against discrimination and arbitrary rule both at home and around the world. We have made great strides, but work remains to be done.

One election does not change who we are as a people. America is exceptional because we are the most diverse nation on earth—different cultures and ideas have come together to make us greater than the sum of our parts. Every citizen has a place in our collective American story that nobody can take from them.

Our Founders included Muslims in their writings on religious freedom, and Muslim Americans have played an important role in shaping our Nation's character since the beginning. They are our athletes and entertainers, public servants and entrepreneurs, scientists and service members.

The America I know is clear-eyed and big-hearted—full of courage and ingenuity. We are defined not by fear, but by hope. Our success has always been rooted in the willingness of our people to look out for one another and to recognize that we are all safer when we work to protect each other's rights. Progress doesn't come easily, and it hasn't always followed a straight line, but I firmly believe that history ultimately moves in the direction of justice, prosperity, freedom, and inclusion—not because it is inevitable, but because ordinary Americans seize the responsibility of citizenship by speaking out and holding our Nation accountable to its highest ideals.

Again, thank you for writing. Whatever challenges we may face, there is no greater form of patriotism than the belief that America is not yet finished and a brighter future lies ahead.

Sincerely,

Letter from President Barack Obama

ACKNOWLEDGEMENTS

Writing your life story – or at least the first 50 years of it - is an extremely arduous process. I had to let the manuscript go for months at a time for multitudinous reasons, the primary one being because many sections have been utterly painful to recreate and in essence -- to re-live. The challenge of mastering the various emotions that were elicited was the main reason why this has taken me in excess of 10 years to complete. Without a doubt and unequivocally, I know that I could not have achieved this goal myself, therefore I am eternally grateful to:

First and foremost, I thank our creator, God Almighty, for giving me the opportunities, strength and steadfast determination to complete this memoir. For without the blessings of Allah and the life given to me, I most certainly would not be here to not only fulfill my life's journey but to be able to write about it too.

For my father, who was the first man to have ever loved me unconditionally and valued me as an equal human being, I am forever indebted. You have taught me that in America, I could reach my highest dreams providing I work hard, speak my truth, stay honest, be true to my word and to have a happy heart. Your mantra, "Never, ever go to sleep angry or unhappy," has been a constant reminder to me that tomorrow is not guaranteed to any of us.

To my mother who has taught me many valuable lessons on how to be as well as how not to be. I realize you did the best you could at the time, with what you had and what you knew. And… I love and forgive you.

To Phil – who is the second man to have loved and valued me unconditionally, even though I came with 'a lot of baggage.' Six months after my father's death I met you and it was love at first sight for both of us. Despite the turmoil and struggles in my personal life as well as within the army ethos, you believed in me, supported me and became the 'silent wind beneath my wings.' Your undying love, patience, and encouragement to pursue my goals has kept me self-confident and energetic to continue to focus on my goals and move-on. After we married, you never hesitated to 'step up' to be the dad I could only dream of for my daughters. And for that, I love and cherish you even more. Similarly, you continued to encourage me to finish this memoir with the same energy and commitment, no matter how long it took.

To my dear daughters who have given me so much love and a valuable purpose in life since the day you were born. I have always felt that my most favorite job in all my life was to be your mother: to love you, care for you, protect you, and raise you the best way I could. My reference to one of you as being the apple of my right eye and the other as the apple of my left eye speaks to the degree of how much I love and honor you. I would sacrifice either eye -- or both -- to attain your safety and well-being. You have both made me so very proud.

To my military superiors and colleagues. I want to express my deepest gratitude for your support, guidance, mentorship, friendship, and camaraderie throughout my military career, whether directly or from a distance. I aspired to model and emulate your leadership styles and endeavored to pass these positive attributes on to junior officers and my subordinates. I feel blessed to have served our country at a time when I had the opportunity to work for you and with you to help make this world a better place for all of us. I have named some of you in my memoir with respect to various narratives and to express my appreciation. I offer my heartfelt thank you to: Lieutenant General Ronald Blanck, Major General Nancy Adams, Major General Gale Pollock, Brigadier General Clara Adams-Ender, Colonel Terris Kennedy, Colonel Sharon Richie, Colonel Sharon Feeney-Jones, Colonel Jeri Graham, Colonel Carol Jones, Colonel Andrea Caldwell, Colonel Niranjan Balliram, Colonel Manuel Delossantos, Colonel John Kugler, Colonel Diane Corcoran, Colonel Jose Melendez, Colonel Warren Todd, Colonel Wilfredo Nieves, Colonel Mary King, Colonel Margarita Aponte, Lieutenant Colonel Doris Leeks, Lieutenant Colonel Phillip Rice, Lieutenant Colonel Carole Burke, Lieutenant Colonel Claire McCormack, Major Judith Ruiz, Major John Schilling, Major Rosamond Sheppard, Major Marilyn Johnson, Major Paula Reynolds, Captain Vien Vanderhoof, Captain Karen Ward, Captain Thuy Tran, Staff Sergeant Marcia Garrett. I can go on and on for there are so many more of you whose work inspired me along the way, and I apologize for leaving anyone out.

To my family members and friends who have in many ways helped me get this book underway. Special thanks to Tante Aidi, my grandmother Erna, my great-grandmother Friederike Bender and my brothers Rick and Jerry for providing important family historical data. Leona and Mary - thank you as well for your love, encouragement and support by mothering and nourishing my soul when I was young, trying to find my way in a new world and helping me piece together valuable information from my youth. My sincere appreciation to Janie (Sr. Gabriele), Sarah and Lawrie, Mr. and Mrs. Hoffman, Norma, Michelle, Karen and Cindy for your support and kindness in helping me along life's path and ultimately get this story told. Again, my apologies for leaving anyone out. Know you have positively impacted my life and my journey to write this memoir.

My deepest gratitude is also extended to President John F. Kennedy, for the inspiration you have given me through your inaugural speech, when I was an immigrant child learning to speak

English and to President Barack Obama for reading part of my story and responding so eloquently in your letter which gave me the motivation and impetus to complete this memoir.

And finally, to my literary team. I extend my deepest gratitude to Emil Toth, for your heartfelt encouragement and for graciously combing through the initial, rough and very wordy draft. My special thanks to Deena Thompson for your careful reading of multiple iterations of this memoir, for your constructive and honest criticism, and for helping me talk through, write, and revise several sections to tell my story in the best way I could. To the team at Book Launchers who helped me develop, edit and finally launch this memoir.

CPSIA information can be obtained
at www.ICGtesting.com
Printed in the USA
FSHW010921240720
71819FS